BALANCING YOUR TEMPERAMENT

Dr Gilbert Childs

SOPHIA BOOKS
London

Sophia Books
Rudolf Steiner Press
51 Queen Caroline Street
London W6 9QL

First published by Sophia Books 1999
(Sophia Books is an imprint of Rudolf Steiner Press)

© Gilbert Childs 1999

The moral right of the author has been asserted under the Copyright, Designs and Patents Act, 1988

All rights reserved. No part of this publication may be reproduced, stored in a retrieval system, or transmitted, in any form or by any means, electronic, mechanical, photocopying, recording or otherwise, without the prior permission of the publishers

A catalogue record for this book is available from the British Library

ISBN 1 85584 067 7

Cover by Andrew Morgan
Typeset by DP Photosetting, Aylesbury, Bucks
Printed and bound in Great Britain by Cromwell Press Limited, Trowbridge, Wiltshire

Contents

	Preface	1
1	The General and the Particular	3
2	Physiognomy and Psychology	22
3	An Artistic View of the World	38
4	A Meditative Approach to Self-knowledge	56
5	Equalizing Positive and Negative	73
6	Smoothing the Mixture	91
7	The Greeks Had a Word for It	110
	Notes and References	119
	Select Bibliography	123

See thou, mine eye,
The Sun's pure rays
In crystal forms of Earth.

See thou, my heart,
The Sun's spirit-power
In Water's surging wave.

See thou, my soul,
The Sun's cosmic will
In quivering gleam of Air.

See thou, my spirit,
The Sun's indwelling God
In Fire's abounding love.

Rudolf Steiner

Preface

Rudolf Steiner once remarked that, ideally at any rate, we should be able to play on our four temperaments as violinists do on the four strings of their violin. However, a more trite but nonetheless appropriate comparison of my own is the notion that we have all been dealt a hand of playing cards in varying proportions of the four temperamental suits, with their actual properties in terms of card values. Needless to say, the manner in which we 'play' our cards in the 'game' of life is entirely our own responsibility.

On a more serious note, however, I have contended, with some justification, that the four human temperaments we are dealing with are powerful archetypal forces, whose essential character and mode of operation I have touched on, if only lightly. I have intentionally reiterated various notions as and when worthwhile and appropriate, and I take full responsibility for the indications offered with regard to the reverberations and resonances that are discernible in the appropriate domains of nature, and their connections and correspondences with the human constitution and condition.

I have also chosen various verses given by Rudolf Steiner, and selected quotations from his other works, with the intention of stimulating and encouraging readers to seek further sources of information and inspiration.

Chapter 1

The General and the Particular

> There is indeed an intermediary between what is brought over from earlier lives and what is provided by heredity. This intermediary possesses the more universal qualities but is at the same time capable of individualization. That which stands midway between the line of heredity and the individual is expressed in the word *temperament*.[1]

Contemporary problems have to be faced

Every human being is unique — in appearance, constitution and character. On the one hand we all bear the stamp of universality, and on the other an unmistakable individuality. As primarily spiritual beings seeking temporary sojourn on earth for purposes of our own development and evolution, we arrive on the material plane with our future in terms of destiny already roughly mapped out. This does not mean that every single event of significance is pre-determined, but rather pre-intended. Whatever else, sooner or later, whatever the circumstances, the laws of karma or self-created destiny must and will be complied with, and particular aims and objectives to this end will certainly have been arrived at in the spiritual worlds before birth.

However, nowadays matters are not so straightforward as they used to be prior to the middle of the twentieth century, because there are now many sources of interference in what used to be reasonably proper procedures. As we are compelled to clothe ourselves in matter in order to exist on earth at all, there is the stream of heredity already available to receive us in terms of race, nation, community and family, all of which we have—ideally—been involved in choosing before birth. I say *ideally* because of the chaotic circumstances which often present themselves in modern times as a direct consequence of the widespread use of reliable means of contraception, the ready availability of abortion techniques, *in vitro* fertilization methods, fertility treatments and so on.

The whole situation, therefore, has been rendered enormously difficult for those incarnating children—or rather their egos—who find their tentative designs thwarted by becoming caught up in such situations. It never could be claimed that our expectations in terms of destiny will be achieved in neat and tidy fashion, as modern medical and surgical practices ensure that occasions will present themselves which require on-the-spot decisions and perhaps even radical changes in strategic planning, even though the overall pattern be retained. However, within the whole framework the capability for us to exercise free will remains.

Thus we are enabled to take our place, whether fully intentioned or not, in the history of the peoples of the world, both as an individual and a member of a particular social group and family. Moreover, we present ourselves as already possessing our own individual history, fashioned and formed according to our own unique karma or self-created destiny, and which necessarily forms part of the history of humankind on our own planet. For better or worse, none of us is obliged to accept our particular circumstances for what they were and are.

How do our temperaments originate?

In the quotation for this chapter, Rudolf Steiner places the matter of reincarnation into the endless argument concerning the ways people think, feel and behave in their adult lives, and this sheds new light upon the old and familiar nature/nurture problem, nowadays called the genes/environment problem. For those who accept the whole notion of self-created destiny and its twin concept of repeated earthly lives the topic is not so problematic as for those who don't. Materialistic scientists are at a distinct disadvantage with regard to this, and will remain so until they come to realize that we are primarily spiritual beings and only secondarily creatures of flesh and blood, and that the ways in which the two principles become integrated marks out our particular 'human nature' which forms such a major factor in the story of our lives as individuals.

Rudolf Steiner often said that the commonly held notion that we are entirely dependent on our parents for all our bodily and psychological characteristics is one of the most unfortunate beliefs ever to be adopted in modern times. We are not entirely dependent on our genes for our appearance and character, for they have strictly to do with heredity and therefore represent only half of the story. If this were the case, then all siblings would be copies of their parents, and this is manifestly not so. The arguments concerning the so-called nature/nurture quandary do not range themselves into either/or categories, but rather both/and correlations.

The real problem lies in the necessity of our incarnating soul-spiritual members and our bodily members, so neatly provided by our parents, to adjust successfully to each other. In effect, this means the integration of our astral body and ego (soul-spiritual principles) with our corporeal members (etheric and physical bodies). Out of this alignment process arises our own unique personality, ideally with the four available temperaments mixed in particular proportion—and reasonably appropriate for future needs and purposes at that.

There is always a dominant temperament and a secondary temperament that is often directly contrary to it, with the other two more or less suffering some degree of subordination or subjection. Since we are not perfect, there is invariably some imbalance. But this is undeniably a blessing in disguise, for our temperaments can be and often are instrumental in furthering our development in overall evolutionary terms. The extent to which we understand 'human nature' is that to which we perceive our own and other people's behaviour in its infinite variety. We may think we know ourselves and our significant others, but this can only ever be part-knowledge; for we human beings are far more complex than even we ourselves realize. For instance, when we sometimes find that we or they are suddenly 'acting out of character' we put it down to our ever-inexplicable 'human nature'.

Just how we manage to 'read' and understand the behaviour of ourselves and others is still something of a mystery, and certainly the whole matter of physiognomy (of the overall physique and not only facial form) is the subject of some debate among psychologists, physiologists and others. Some researchers limit physiognomy to facial features, whereas most investigators consider the entire body build. It must be said that human features mostly reflect body build. For example, overweight people invariably have chubby faces, and tall, thin individuals usually possess long thin noses and narrow features. For the most part overall harmony prevails.

The fact is that there are four temperaments, but orthodoxy maintains that there are only three body types (somatotypes), and a full discussion concerning the impossibilities surrounding this problem—and the likely solution to it—can be found elsewhere.[2] This principle of fourfoldness is of course one of many to be found in both outer and human nature, and as a framework for several easily discernible phenomenological patterns. The four elements of ancient Greek science (Fire, Air, Water, Earth) spring immediately to mind, as does our own fourfold constitution which corresponds respectively to the human ego, astral body, etheric body and physical body. Needless to say, there are archetypal agencies at work behind all these principles, but such connections are too complex to be discussed here. Nevertheless, various indications are to be found scattered throughout this book as convenient and appropriate.

We're all the same – only different

The ancient doctrine that all human beings can be somehow categorized into four psychological types—and indeed corresponding body types—is now widely regarded as unscientific and therefore untenable. However, there are valid grounds for contending that as a general principle such precepts are firmly rooted not only in tradition but in everyday experience also. The situation is one that is frequently met with in these days of scientific and academic specialisms; in this case it is a matter of psychologists, biologists and others not being able to see the wood for the trees, thus sparking the question: when is an 'expert' not an expert?

Generally speaking, science sticks firmly to the practice of evaluating everything quantitatively—everything must be counted, weighed, measured. However, certain areas of knowledge are best explored by employing qualitative methodologies. Where human nature and the four temperaments are concerned much is necessarily involved that is almost impossible to measure, and therefore incalculable in exact terms. A sick person's temperature can be ascertained to a fraction of a degree, but how can the look in their eyes—of alarm, anxiety, pain, despair, hope—be measured?

In reality, it is practically impossible to coerce that which lies within the realm of the widely incalculable into that of the narrowly calculable. Where the human temperaments are concerned, and indeed the whole human constitution, there are so many variables which fall into the incalculable category that the precision and exactness demanded by researchers into matters psychological cannot and does not apply. In short, they have been attempting the impossible, and this is why all reference to the temperaments in modern scientific literature is cursory and very often undeservingly derisory.

All this being so, the least that can be said is that the doctrine of the four temperaments has stood the test of time, whereas the work of such researchers as Kretschmer, Cattell, Sheldon, Vernon, and even Eysenck, who made a brave attempt at exploring their complexities, has for the most part been laid aside.[3] Their efforts were rendered impossible of real achievement because of their tendency to force the principles governing the temperaments into moulds that were not fitting. Moreover, their faith in the 'factor analysis' approach was unfounded, for they invariably attempted to introduce too many behavioural or personality factors—and at the same time, of course, their essential incalculability. Failure was inevitable, if only for the fact that various workers in the personality factor field attempted to reconcile four temperaments with three body-types.[4]

The word *temperament* derives from the Latin word *temperamentum*, 'a mixing (of the humours)' from *temporare*, to mingle, and of course it is true that a person's temperament comprises all four temperaments, but mixed in due proportion as uniquely proper to that individual. According to medieval thinking, these four humours were directly associated with our body fluids, namely, blood, phlegm, choler (yellow bile) and black bile, which in turn give rise respectively to sanguine, phlegmatic, choleric and melancholic characteristics. Thus we all are made of the same ingredients, but different in proportion and scale. It is barely conceivable that such an eminent figure as the philosopher Immanuel Kant (1724–1804) was adamant that each individual possessed one, and only one, 'cardinal humour' or main temperament; and more recently the pioneer psychologist and physiologist Wilhelm Wundt (1832–1920) was of the same opinion.

Usually, everyone possesses a main or dominant temperament, although more often than not it is possible to discern subsidiary characteristics which can readily be associated with a secondary temperament. But as we possess all four in greater or lesser proportion this leaves two more of lesser influence, and quite often it is easy, by a process of elimination, to determine which temperament is weakest. However, the more 'even-tempered' we are in the true sense of our being 'well-tempered', the more likely we are to be *good-tempered*. We are fortunate if our main temperament is not too dominant, for then it is easier for us to make use of all four temperaments as circumstances require, and this to the best all-round advantage to ourselves and our neighbours.

The fourfoldness of the natural world

Rudolf Steiner pointed out that the four human temperaments are closely associated with our fourfold nature, and for present purposes it is necessary to be clear about this, for it is possible to present an elegant and valid model of the human being as such. Greek science saw nature in fourfold terms: Fire, Air, Water and Earth. Everything that was connected with heat and high temperatures was represented by the element of Fire, and characterized for instance by the heat of the sun and the warmth of our blood, as well as ordinary flames. The element of Air was associated with everything that is gaseous in character and constitution, just as everything that manifested a fluid nature was categorized as Water, whether the liquid be actual water, wine, juices — whatever flowed was Water. The element of Earth stood for all substances that were solid, and possessed the typical qualities of resistance, form and weight associated with such materials or objects. Apart from rocks, stones and the more obvious solid stuff, material such as bones, shells and most metals were similarly classified.

All this seems sensible enough for the times, and of course the general principles still hold. Looking around us in the world, we are soon able to observe that there are comparatively inert and lifeless substances everywhere, such as soil, stones and minerals, which do not change their outward natures to any appreciable degree. Sandstone can be hammered and ground into small particles, which still retain their hardness and other 'earthly' qualities. Such substances, which are classified in terms of chemical elements by modern science, interact with one another in a purely chemical fashion, or by the agency of such physical forces as frost, heat, friction and so on. They may change their chemical formulae, and even their nature according to the Greek way of classification, into liquids, gases or even fire as such. Nevertheless, whatever kind of change or metamorphosis ensues it is always effected by reason of purely chemical or physical activity, combining to form a different compound or mixture by whatever means. The main criterion is that whatever the product it will remain utterly devoid of *life*.

Our corporeal nature

It is of course not difficult to discern the association between Earth in the Greek sense with our physical-material body, for it obtains its constitution in mineral and chemical terms from the very earth beneath our feet. These material substances are taken up by energies or forces which exhibit all the qualities we associate with *life*, a fundamental principle in nature. Pre-scientific natural philosophy, as might be expected, was well aware of this process, and the notion of *élan vital*, or 'vital force' was posited in explanation. This was considered quite rightly to account for the difference between inert chemical substances as static earthly matter and their appearance in all members of the plant world, which had extracted them from the earth with the help of light and heat, air and moisture.

It is evident that the active presence of the other three 'elements', namely, Fire, Air and Water, working together, is necessary for this life-process, itself invisible and undetectable by any of our senses, to function. Furthermore they operate in an orderly, organized way, so that we can say with all certainty that every *organism* necessarily possesses an etheric body as well as a material one. When circumstances are present which allow the three elements to work as an integrated whole or unit, it is seen to be an entity imbued with life, which organism not only manifests in *space* but also endures through *time*.

The life-principle thus seen to be at work in all living beings, whether plant, animal or human, is well known to spiritual science, and is often called the *etheric body* or 'life-body', sometimes referred to by Rudolf Steiner as the 'formative-forces body', which is a more graphic term. An immediately discernible characteristic of this etheric body is that it has strong connections with the factor of duration, for it takes time for any organism to build, form, organize, bring to maturity, and make preparations to ensure the continuation of its species by means of some kind of propagation process after their 'time is up'.

Etheric forces are always associated with the presence of water, and it is well known that the human being is actually composed mostly of water—hence the medium is there for the action of the functions of healing, repair and regeneration of the cells. The etheric body is therefore responsible for providing the patterns of growth, shape, form and function of all bodily organs, including of course those of reproduction. Although every cell in the body is renewed at varying rates, its structure, whether healthy or not, retains its original shape and form, faithfully preserved by the etheric organization.

Thus an entity which possesses an 'etheric' body possesses the ability to grow and reproduce in accordance with its kind, with its particular family, genus and species; that is to say, it represents the *life-principle* identifiable by its ability to take up and organize matter. Of whatever disposition we are, the characteristics which make it up are firmly rooted in our etheric body, our 'formative-forces body'. Its presence is also characterized by the principle of *rhythmical repetition* evident in whatever organism is shaped by it. Obviously, when it is no longer possible for this life-principle to maintain itself for whatever reason, the organism concerned 'dies'.

In the plant kingdom a life of permanent sleep exists, as no tree, shrub, plant or vegetable is conscious in the way that animals and humans are. They do not possess sense organs and nervous system as sentient creatures do, and cannot feel pain or emotions of any kind. Vibrant with inner life-processes, plants have no means of locomotion, and any spatial movements in leaves, flowers and fruit, or indeed the whole organism, are invariably due to outer agencies which are utterly mechanical, and not made as the result of conscious wish or choice. For instance, the manner in which the 'jaws' of the Venus' fly-trap close may *appear* to involve some kind of sensing activity, but investigation confirms that this cannot be and is not the case.

Our astral or 'consciousness' body

Esoteric tradition, confirmed by modern spiritual science, posits an answer to the mystery of *consciousness*, still regarded as such by modern science, which is unable to provide any satisfactory solution to this riddle. Philosophers are faced with the situation of consciousness having to examine itself, and this feat is not easy to accomplish. When most people think of consciousness, they usually 'have in mind' our ordinary waking consciousness, that is to say, our mental processes integral to our faculties of thinking, feeling and willing.

We all know what it is like to experience the endless flow of sense-impressions which form the overwhelming proportion of our waking lives. Our normal waking consciousness involves to a great extent a continuous stream of impressions that pour in via our sense organs—sight, hearing, smell, taste and so on—and we rely heavily on these as we go about our daily activities. But even when we are resting, perhaps sitting or lying down in a quiet room, with our eyes closed and receiving barely a single sense-impression, our mind—our consciousness—is still very active with thoughts and ideas, memories and reflections, hopes and fears, plans for the immediate and distant future, and so forth.

Our mental life is usually very active the whole time we are awake; rarely, if ever, is our mind a total blank. Earlier on I referred to our 'consciousness-system' or sentient system as a 'body', but this does not of course refer to anything solid or material. Our sense-organs, however, and the central nervous system and brain which are connected with them are of course constituted of living tissues which do consist of matter, and it is justifiable to refer to the whole organization and structure as a 'body'. Of course our thoughts and feelings along with our sense-perceptions are undetectable by means of our physiological senses, but the fact they do comprise an organized structure warrants the use of the term 'body'.

Our ego as sense of self

It must be understood at the outset that the ego as posited here is not to be confused with the 'ego' of orthodox psychology, which regards it as merely one of three divisions of the mind, that which serves as the organized conscious mediator between the person and reality. In this theory, the other two mental components are the 'id', which is completely unconscious and is the source of psychic energy derived from instinctual drives, and the 'super-ego', which is considered to be only partly conscious and is developed from child–parent relationships and reflects social rules, approximating to what is usually characterized as conscience.

Spiritual science affirms that in addition to physical, etheric and astral bodies every human being possesses a fourth member: the ego or 'I'. The ego represents the factor of individualization, that which guarantees the uniqueness of every man, woman and child. The word 'I' is unique in that no person can use it to designate another, and represents the 'Higher Self' in each one of us, equating in approximate terms to the human spirit. The ego is the co-ordinating and initiating principle, which as a constant observer preserves the past by virtue of memory, experiences the present, and by its agency for action helps to determine the future for ourselves and others. It is the only permanent element in every human being, and as such guarantees their immortality.

The soul, which may justifiably be equated to the astral body, experiences the material world through the bodily senses on the one hand and is influenced and motivated by the spirit-filled ego on the other, to which the soul passes on the fruits of its experiences and eventually perishes. This must be so; the body dies upon the departure from it, for whatever reason, of the etheric body which sustains it. Considering the economy of nature on a universal scale, as at the death of the human physical-mineral organism its chemical components are returned to the earth, either by natural decomposition or as ashes after cremation, so the etheric body returns to the etheric world from whence it was drawn. In similar fashion, the part of the astral body that has not been transformed by the ego also undergoes a kind of 'decomposition' process, and is returned to the astral world. Hence, with the death of the corporeal nature (physical body plus etheric body), the soul (astral body) which dwelt in it also in due course passes away.

Correspondences with the temperaments

There are definite correlations between our physical-mineral (sensory) organization and our soul-spiritual (supersensory) organization, and brief introductory remarks are appropriate at this stage:

Principle	Bodily correlation	Temperament
Ego	Blood (warmth)	Choleric
Astral body	Brain/nerves	Sanguine
Etheric	Glands/fluids	Phlegmatic
Physical	Bones/mineral nature	Melancholic

In the case of the ego it is not so much the blood itself that is implied here, but rather the *warmth* that is associated with it, and hence the element of Fire. The astral body is the bearer of our consciousness, and this attribute is readily associated with our sense-organs and the network of nerves which serves the brain. It is noteworthy that the Greek word *pneuma* can mean air or breath, life or spirit, and these attributes are all associated with the qualities of soul that characterize our astral principle. The bodily fluids secreted via our glandular system have obvious connotations with the element of Water, and hence are the vehicle of the etheric principle. Interesting in this regard is the fact that the etheric body, as has already been mentioned, is closely associated with all that is watery, and the 'humours' referred to earlier are of course fluid in consistency. Earth represents resistance and weight, solidity and gravity, which are all qualities traditionally associated with the melancholic temperament.

It is important also to realize that the ruling temperament has different associations in the case of children, although the actual temperamental characteristics are in no way altered. A simple table makes matters clear:

Ruling temperament	As child	As adult
Melancholic	Ego	Physical body
Choleric	Astral body	Ego
Sanguine	Etheric body	Astral body
Phlegmatic	Physical body	Etheric body

It is also important at this point to mention that parents, teachers and significant others should remember never to work against a child's temperament, but always with it. Experience has shown that it is better never to urge or try to persuade melancholic children to 'snap out of it', or attempt to amuse them by telling jokes in the hope of cheering them up. It is far better to commiserate with them, and make them realize that they are not the only ones who have troubles. Similarly, it is unwise to rant and rave when choleric children throw a tantrum or make some kind of destructive mischief; remain calm and cool, and don't, so to speak, feed the flames. Make sure that sanguine children are continuously occupied, for even they will eventually get tired and will not 'occupy' you. As for phlegmatic children, show them that you can be as disinterested as they, but surreptitiously encourage them to get acquainted with others who have interests or 'crazes' which are of consuming interest to them.

Our subjective and objective natures

Rudolf Steiner associated form and force with the physical body, life and movement with the etheric body, and consciousness with the astral body.[5] It is clear that just as our physical and etheric bodies together constitute our *corporeal* make-up, they can with justification be designated our *objective* nature. We have little control over their essential functions, which are performed in ways so automated that if their requirements are adequately met in terms of food, warmth and similar 'animal comforts' their existence is taken very much for granted. We feel that our corporeal nature belongs to us, that we 'have' it rather than 'are' it. Hence we habitually say, if something is amiss or especially noticeable about our corporeal nature, that we 'have' a cough, sore thumb, double chin or freckles, as if these conditions are somehow outside us, which in a certain sense they are.

Our astral body and ego together comprise our *soul-spiritual* constitution, our *subjective* principle. Where feelings and thoughts are concerned, we are so closely bound up with them that we actually identify ourselves with them. Hence we often say respectively that we 'are' miserable, jealous, upset or delighted, and perhaps uncertain, doubtful, honest or confident. It can readily be seen from this that we actually possess two sets of temperaments, two of which are objective in nature, namely, the melancholic and phlegmatic (physical and etheric principles respectively), and two which are essentially subjective, namely, the sanguine and choleric (astral body and ego respectively). We are indeed very fortunate individuals if we are able fully to integrate our subjective and objective natures, for then we are more likely to be truly *temperate* in our whole being, well-balanced and equable human beings, and this is of course a worthy aim.

What has world evolution to do with the temperaments?

It would be fair to say that the thinking and attitudes of modern scientists, including biologists, physiologists and psychologists, are thoroughly materialistic, and for the most part essentially Darwinistic. They accept no other view than that the universe came about as the result of a 'big bang', which occurred at some unthinkably remote time in the past, and that the existence of *Homo sapiens* has come about only a relatively short time ago. We ourselves are deemed to have originated from the coming together of the requisite proportions of certain proteins and other elements which were present in the primeval ooze which resulted in the formation of living organisms from which we have evolved over aeons. This is the orthodox view which is widely accepted—but as fact rather than hypothesis.

From the point of view of spiritual science, this notion is about as valid as regarding the earth as being flat, which equates with the notion that matter is the basis of all phenomena, and that what is supersensory has its origins in the sensory. It assumes that life arises from the lifeless and the dynamic from the static, irrespective of the law that like arises only from like. Rudolf Steiner often pointed out that today's materialistic scientists will never understand matter until they realize that in matter the spiritual is continuously at work.

According to orthodox teaching, the origins of both the universe and ourselves are the result of chance events; but science itself rests squarely on the principle of causality, that is to say, every effect must have a prior cause. The fact that no cause for the 'big bang' has been discovered or even postulated does not conform with this basic scientific law. Furthermore, no reason for the existence of life itself has been determined, and the contention that it is solely for the continuation of life by means of propagation of the various species according to the principles of natural selection is not valid as evidence, proof or verdict.

There can be no argument that evolutionary processes have taken place, and that these are set to continue. The law of change, of continuous metamorphosis, is seen to be at work everywhere, at a rate and on a scale appropriate to all situations and circumstances. The evolutionary model posited by anthroposophical spiritual science can be seen to be eminently reasonable and orderly if approached without prejudice or bias. Further acquaintance with its principles lead on to certain patterns becoming discernible which appear sound and reasonable, and moreover not only mutually supportive but also in full accord with the realities of our own existence and those of our environment.

Rudolf Steiner asserted that as far as spiritual science is concerned with the nature of human beings there is no difference between theory and practice. Orthodox science denies the existence of spirit, so theories involving the notions of psychologists such as those mentioned earlier were bound to fail by reason of their sheer inadequacy. Spiritual science is on secure ground when it posits a fourfold membering of the human being, as this is positively archetypal in character and cannot be refuted.

Our oldest and indeed our most 'perfect' vehicle is that of the human physical body itself, which has its origin in the evolutionary periods traditionally related to the Days of Creation and reflected in the names of the days of the week as Saturday, Sunday and Monday. These are known as Old Saturn, Old Sun, Old Moon, and together with the current Earth evolution mark the acquisition in consecutive fashion of our etheric body, astral body and ego respectively, as follows:[6]

Evolutionary stage	Constituent vehicle(s)	Kingdom of nature
Old Saturn	Physical	Mineral
Old Sun	Physical, etheric	Plant
Old Moon	Physical, etheric, astral	Animal
Earth	Physical, etheric, astral, ego	Human

These four stages are faithfully reflected in the four kingdoms of nature clearly evident in the world about us, and also in ourselves as representing a kind of conglomeration of all four kingdoms. Correspondences and correlations do not stop there, as we can see:

Element	Vehicle mainly concerned	Temperament
Earth	Physical body	Melancholic
Water	Etheric body	Phlegmatic
Air	Astral body	Sanguine
Fire	Ego	Choleric

Whereas the models comprising the somewhat arbitrary factors chosen by orthodox psychologists are seen to be unconvincing, growing acquaintance with those appearing in the tables inspire confidence by their very factors of cohesion and consistency of nature and function. Their archetypal nature ensures their reliability, and this serves to underpin the whole tradition of the four temperaments, the understanding of which is as much an art as it is a science, as we shall see in due course.

Chapter 2

Physiognomy and Psychology

> Let me have men about me that are fat;
> Sleek-headed men, and such as sleep o'nights;
> Yond' Cassius has a lean and hungry look;
> He thinks too much: such men are dangerous.[1]

The problem of body types

It is clear from the quotation above, and indeed from his works in general, that Shakespeare was skilled in physiognomy, the 'art of discovering temperament and character from outward appearance', and unmatched in his perception and understanding of human nature. The doctrine of the four temperaments was well known to the Greek physician Galen (*c.* 130–*c.* 200) and to others long before that, perhaps even as far back as Hippocrates (*c.*460–*c.*377 BC), the so-called father of medicine. Modern psychologists, however, have little time for any such typology as that of the temperaments, which they consider too nebulous to be taken seriously. It is very doubtful, for instance, that the latest 'ology' in this area to have sprouted, namely, *Personology*, will be taken seriously either.

It was obvious then, as it is now, that there are basically two somatotypes, or categories of body build; for in this respect people are, roughly speaking, either short and broad (eurymorphic), or tall and slender (leptomorphic). These two classes correspond neatly in that we have the cholerics and phlegmatics, who are usually stocky in build, and the sanguines and melancholics, who are invariably slight in figure and form. Moreover, in many important respects, as will be seen from the numerous indications given throughout this book, the four temperaments can, with equal validity, be classified into other pairings which are definitely taken seriously nowadays—for example, the introvert/extrovert grouping. This grouping accurately identifies the two main somatotypes respectively as the eurymorphic cholerics and phlegmatics, and the leptomorphic sanguines and melancholics. In other words, cholerics are stockily built extroverts, sanguines are slightly built extroverts, phlegmatics are stubby introverts, and melancholics are tall and thin introverts.

Of course there are variations, frequently on account of the effects of the secondary temperament, but as a rough guide it is reliable enough. The question is bound to arise as to just why such an art as physiognomy is as valid as it is, for it has its limitations and cannot claim to be an exact science. We are indeed all the same, only different, but to contend that 'it's all in the genes' is merely saying that a spade is a spade is a spade, and there are all kinds of factors involved which modern researchers do not take into account. For personality assessment they mainly rely on more or less sophisticated psychometric techniques which, however, share the limited value of snapshot photographs. They cannot take into account tendencies that are generating within a person over the longer term, as their characteristics develop throughout their lifetime.

However, ordinary observation will confirm Steiner's important assertion that whatever the dominant temperament of an individual it is overlaid in childhood by sanguine propensities, and in youth and early adulthood by choleric tendencies, and therefore undeniably extroverted in disposition. During middle life people incline towards introversion, when melancholic traits appear, and in old age a kind of phlegmatic indifference and resignation is usually the prevailing mood. Thus the willing/feeling inclinations of youth gradually give way to those of feeling/thinking in old age.

Matters of body/soul configurations

We know that our temperaments are established in our etheric body, and Rudolf Steiner averred that the 'various members of our etheric body are differentiated according to the different temperaments: the upper part is inclined to the melancholic temperament, the central part alternates between phlegmatic and sanguine, and the lower part is inclined to the choleric'.[2] In this statement, made in 1913, we are already able to discern indications he made several years later, when he published his findings concerning mankind's fundamentally threefold nature.[3] Briefly, he pointed out that our head, with its brain and supporting nerves-sense system, serves our faculties of thinking; that our rhythmic system of heart and lungs, which occupies our chest cavity, serves our life of feeling; and that our metabolic-limbs system sustains our forces of willing.

Just as our solid, physical-material body exists principally in the element of space, our etheric body endures through that of time. In our corporeal being we are indeed 'dwellers all in time and space', and the two vehicles abide synchronously and coincidentally. As long as an organism is alive, the physical and etheric vehicles must be sufficiently well integrated to allow of its continuation in the vital state. Should either of these two principles for reason of terminal illness or severe injury find it impossible to maintain this bonding, partition occurs and what we call death ensues. Thereupon, the mineral body returns its constituent substances to the material world, and the etheric body its particular forces to the etheric world diffused throughout the cosmos.

From this it would be reasonable to deduce that, with regard to the factor of time, the mineral body during life sustains close association with the etheric body, and hence our powers of thinking, ideation and memory. These processes have an obvious correlation with the head and its supporting network of nerves and senses, so the melancholic temperament may with some justification be regarded as being concerned mainly with what is *past*. Our rhythmic system is undeniably affiliated to our whole life of feeling and, in terms of temperament, to all that exhibits connections with sanguine tendencies (outer concerns) and phlegmatic proclivities (inner concerns). These are unfailingly expressed in the here and now, and therefore involve mainly with what is going on in the *present*. Our metabolic-limbs system is manifestly related to the choleric temperament, and by inference to the will with its propensity for *future action*.[4]

Rudolf Steiner stated that for melancholics past experiences resonate within their inner nature for a long time, and they often have difficulty in 'letting them go'. Sanguines alternate between past and present considerations, whereas phlegmatics float along steadily with the flow of time. Cholerics, however, have the tendency to resist the approach of future time.[5] These indications in themselves give much food for thought and contemplation according to individual needs and circumstances.

It is clear from all this that our basic soul-faculties of thinking, feeling and willing are closely associated with our corresponding physical-material constitution. Here we encounter the problem of *what determines what* in respect of this typical 'chicken and egg' puzzle, involving as it does the whole concept of physiognomy and its validity. Does our bodily conformation or somatotype determine, or at least influence, our psychological characteristics, or vice versa? The answer seems to depend on each individual person's capability when faced with the necessary task of integrating their soul-spiritual nature, which they have brought with them from the spiritual realms at birth, with their bodily conformation provided by the workings of heredity.

It is important to bear in mind that our main and subsidiary temperaments, regardless of their characteristics, are entrenched in our etheric body. They are, in a very real sense built into us, into our very constitution; and this is why certain bodily characteristics are manifest in our very physiognomy according to temperament. The essentially *formative* function of the etheric body ensures this; for in a very real sense the physical and etheric bodies are fully identified with each other. This is why the melancholic and phlegmatic temperaments are so much alike in many ways. For example, people who have either of these as their main temperament share the same qualities characteristic of passivity, conventionalism, restraint, discretion, conservatism, and even narrow-mindedness.

The matter of actual body build is an interesting one, for whereas melancholic people are in the main leptomorphic (tall and thin), phlegmatics are eurymorphic (short and thickset). It is as if the solid (bony) nature of melancholics constitutes a concentration of matter in a centrifugal way, whereas the phlegmatic build is suggestive of centripetal, expansive influences. This view is supported by the fact that the forces of *gravity* are strongly evident in the melancholic physiognomy, and those of *levity* in that of phlegmatic types.

This assertion in turn is underpinned by the notion that melancholics are related to the earthly forces, whereas

Physiognomy and Psychology 27

phlegmatics possess rather a cosmic nature. Phlegmatics live, as it were, in their body fluids, more particularly in their glandular system, and in this respect represent a comparatively early stage of human development. The bony system, centrally placed as it is in the organism, is the very last physiological structure to be 'precipitated', hardened and fully formed from mineral substances, and which remains mainly lifeless. The presence of bone marrow with its blood-forming propensities represents the exact polar opposite of the blood, which is the most spiritual—or *spiritualized*—of all our organs.

As might be expected, this polarity is reflected in the heat of the blood, with its connotations of fire and choler, and the solidly mineral, earthy skeleton which does not possess blood-vessels, lymphatic support, glands and suchlike, and is relatively 'cold', as melancholics commonly are in a soul-spiritual sense. The blood is characteristic of much that is Luciferic in nature, and the skeleton much of what is Ahrimanic. Melancholic folk, weighed down as they are by Ahrimanic gravity, would certainly benefit both themselves and others by taking steps to engage the Luciferic forces which reside in their blood, and warm themselves through and through with them to their very bones. This should result in their becoming more compassionate, benevolent and charitable, with sympathetic and empathetic qualities far beyond the innate capabilities of the other temperaments. Their innate qualities of fellow-feeling, kindness, consideration, tenderness and so on, which they have hitherto lavished *upon themselves* in an egotistical way, will then be shared in ever greater measure with others. Sooner or later they will take on properties of expansiveness, generosity and magnanimity, much after the fashion of Scrooge after his change of heart.[6]

The temperaments and their polarities

In the case of the temperaments that share the qualities of activity, liberalism, progressiveness, permissiveness and broadmindedness, again we are faced with a kind of inner polarity. Typical cholerics will get the task done even if it kills them, whilst sanguines will walk away from the job upon (early) lack of interest. Again, we have one eurymorphic (choleric) and one leptomorphic (sanguine) type; but as both strongly incline towards the soul-spiritual in nature, there is little to 'anchor' them. It is therefore not surprising to find that if a person possesses a main temperament that is identifiable as being in the one category, he or she may well have a secondary temperament that belongs to the other. A good instance of this is the choleric/ melancholic pairing, which gives rise to the typical manic-depressive type of behaviour, or the sanguine-melancholic mixture, resulting in swings of mood between optimism and pessimism. Contraction and expansion, reductionism and pluralism, and even weeping and laughing are only a few examples of what can, respectively, be said to be Ahrimanic or Luciferic in character, but as always a degree of equilibrium is capable of being brought about.

We all possess characteristics of the phlegmatic element in due proportion to our other temperaments, all of which go to make up our own individuality. As mentioned earlier every single temperamental quality is rooted in the etheric body, irrespective of the fact that, in the main, choleric traits are essentially expressible through the heat of our blood, sanguine qualities through the airy nature of our rhythmic system (lungs and heart), phlegmatic propensities via our glandular system, and melancholic attributes by means of all we manifest in terms of rigidity and solidity, namely, our skeleton.

These are typically associated with the traditional elemental characteristics of Fire, Air, Water and Earth respectively. In a fully functioning human being, all these qualities and attributes are necessary for their smooth operation, that is to say, everything must work in harmony to the extent that all functions are co-ordinated so as to impart the sense or feeling of selfhood, unity and wholeness. It is the paramount function of any etheric organization to achieve harmony above all, and the temperament most characteristic of this trait is without doubt the phlegmatic.

Rudolf Steiner advised that stability, imperturbability and equanimity are highly desirable qualities to cultivate in all circumstances of life, and essential for steady progress along any path of personal or esoteric development. Mainly because of this, but also because phlegmatic people are in any case highly sensitive to changes within their own constitution, bodily and soul-spiritual, they—provided their interest in spiritual development is sufficiently aroused, of course—are already at an advantage in that they possess many of the qualities that are prerequisite for esoteric training, such as patience, perseverance and powers of application to the task. Steiner, who could never be accused of any kind of bias, asserted that 'the phlegmatic type whose soul develops is therefore the best material for serious anthroposophical development'.[7]

It is noteworthy that in this he was careful to say 'the phlegmatic type *whose soul develops...*', and this is of course true of all the other temperaments, each of which has its particular drawbacks. The qualities of endurance and reliability, and the tendencies towards maintaining order, regularity and rhythm are of course also characteristic of all true phlegmatics as well as the etheric forces *per se*. Whether such attributes are exercised to good effect or not is very much an individual affair. It is all too often the case that phlegmatic people give themselves over to a life of ease and comfort, indifferent to and unconcerned with everything that does not serve their appetite for whatever is pleasant and self-satisfying. They all too easily 'let themselves go' and give way to their own selfish desires, careless of all else.

And so it is with the other three temperaments. For example, the 'undeveloped' sanguine is prone to become a scatterbrain, superficial and frivolous, passing their days in a kind of frenetic pursuit of the novel, the alluring and the enchanting. However, if their temperament matures they are quick to pick up ideas and to see opportunities for good. Then their inbuilt social conscience, and perhaps even a long-term interest, may become engaged, which in turn effects a certain balancing-out in terms of temperament.

Similarly, 'primitive' choleric people, bossy and demanding, who charge around giving orders and blame everyone but themselves when things go wrong, may well, after a lifetime of hard work and effort, develop into benevolent and considerate people who look upon the faltering efforts of others with kindly and understanding eyes, perhaps offering help, advice—and even a loan or gift. Melancholic folk, well acquainted themselves with real or imaginary grief and woe—and whilst at the callow, undeveloped stage making sure at the same time that others are also thus acquainted, of course—may well grow into compassionate, empathetic, self-sacrificing people who rarely let an opportunity to be helpful go by.

Thus we can see that developed phlegmatic people in particular, who have a powerful propensity towards finding their own level, and exhibit evenness in character, behaviour and outlook, at the same time knowingly or unknowingly strive towards *balance*—and that is always to be desired. It is worth remembering that our etheric body is also our 'time-body'. As it is also our 'life-body', it is responsible for everything to do with our conception, growth and development to maturity, and beyond to old age. Eventually it departs as mysteriously as it arrived, and what we know as death ensues. Our etheric forces have everything to do with *formative* processes, which extend to the activating of our powers of memory and recall, our capability to form ideas and concepts, and indeed everything that belongs to our mental life.

Thus 'development' of our main and subsidiary temperaments is certainly possible, and this necessarily implies metamorphosis and change. Rudolf Steiner once likened such development throughout life to the hands of a clock. Our more mobile and changeable astral body, as largely reflecting our personality, is represented by the minute hand, whereas the slower pace of the hour hand is rather indicative of our less tractable etheric body, which brings about changes in our character at a much slower pace. As virtually synonymous with our soul, our astral body is perfectly constituted to employ its considerable powers with regard to our faculties of thinking, feeling and willing. This capability, together with its fundamental characteristic of swinging between what to us is regarded as sympathetic or antipathetic, is very effective as an exploratory or investigatory 'tool' for exploiting our experiences to advantage.

During an average lifetime such changes can even affect the principle that is the most uncompromising or unyielding of all, and that is of course our physical-material body. This is easily apparent during the later years of life, when the lines and furrows that invariably appear on the facial features of elderly people can often tell much concerning their particular life-experiences. Close observation of their general bodily configuration, habitual gestures and established behavioural patterns can also be very revealing in this regard.

A strong ego is a must

We do not usually change our basic constitution as we mature and develop; rather—ideally, at any rate—do we ennoble our primary temperament and attempt to exercise our secondary and other temperaments as best we can. This is all part of the process of balancing them out, thus achieving a degree of equilibrium, and hence stability and firmness. This in turn implies a further requirement, namely, the possession of a strong ego as the centre from which to direct our lives.

By virtue of the memories of our past welcome and unwelcome experiences, our triumphs and disasters, our successes and failures, we are able to reflect on them and, by taking as detached a viewpoint as possible, ponder them and come to judgements about the wisdom or otherwise of our actions. All this, it is important to remember, is a crucial task of our ego. Generally speaking, the further behind us such experiences are, the more sound and accurate will be our evaluation of them. This, of course, is how we learn, and how 'character development' takes place; for what we learn from past experiences is generally very useful for determining future courses of action. We may feel that we are 'better' or 'worse' persons as a result of these experiences, for making such moral judgements and assessments of our progress or otherwise is the natural thing to do.

It is therefore our 'ego', referred to by many people as our 'higher being', which observes, co-ordinates and evaluates the experiences we have lived through, and invariably seeks the reasons for their occurrence. Reflections on how they are likely to influence future happenings are very often accompanied by feelings of determination and resolve to 'become a better person'. Ideally, such feelings should inspire altruism, and so give incentive for unselfish deeds and actions. Changes in personal behaviour for the betterment of self and society often result in 'inner peace' as well as an unwavering desire to continue striving for the common good.

Many psychologists go as far as calling what most people are conscious of as a guiding principle, this indefinite if seemingly unidentifiable concept of a 'higher self', our 'ego-ideal', by which we set ourselves increasingly higher standards as we progress towards some ideal or goal. However, this term is inadequate in that an ideal, even an 'ego-ideal', must be deemed to be held by a separate agent, and this is of course the ego itself. The ideal or goal to which our ego addresses itself may be something as trivial as reducing our weight or golf handicap, but the concept that is always unmistakably present is that of improvement, betterment, even perfection in whatever it is we have in mind—in other words, the will to *win*.

Some psychologists contend that what urges people to make themselves better in terms of morality has to do with standards of behaviour which we were expected to achieve as children, manifesting in later life as conscience. This may well be so to a certain extent, but it leaves no appreciation of the fact that all the experiences of childhood events, including admonishment, reproach and blame, and praise, encouragement and correction, must have been subject to a certain degree of interpretation, organization and co-ordination by some kind of integrating agency.

This agency strives to ensure that they do not remain as a mass of isolated or undifferentiated complexes and neuroses, but to make sense of whatever is experienced. We should be justified in calling this agency, this higher principle within us which abides whilst the body necessarily records the changes wrought by the passage of time, our ego — that which maintains our sense of essential selfhood throughout our lives, from infancy to old age, in which the faculty of memory plays such a vital part. So it is the ego that observes, monitors and co-ordinates, which provides a basis for our 'ego-ideal' that urges us on unceasingly to make ever more progress in whatever field of activity we choose, and which ensures that we set our sights progressively higher as objective after objective is achieved.

Do you have a strong ego?

As it is the ego which asserts itself, it is reasonable to assume that, where moral perfection, social responsibility or advancement in the spiritual life is the aim, it is responsible also for our conscience as serving as a point of reference for our deeds and our ideals. It is the ego by which we assess our progress, or lack of it, by pondering past triumphs and disasters as objectively and critically as we can. If little or no advancement is made, the urge to arrange matters so that this may become possible appears unbidden, and without prompting from others. The incentive to raise our sights appears, and with it a fresh determination and resolve to achieve our new goal.

Obviously, the stronger our ego the more likely we are to succeed in our efforts. But what is meant by 'strong ego'? Individuals who appear to have a 'strong personality' may not necessarily possess a strong ego. They may well be empowered to wield authority, and to give orders to everyone but themselves, but they may in fact have a weak ego. Thrusting, ambitious individuals, whose drive and determination have made them multimillionaires, may owe their success to being cunning, ruthless, opportunistic or shrewd in their dealings, motivated and inspired by the prospect of riches and a luxurious life-style—in other words, thoroughly selfish characters, thoroughgoing egotists.

A striking comparison with such people can be made with the nature of young children, who are the most thoroughgoing egotists of all. They behave with the most blatant self-interest—quite instinctively, of course—and yet they do not 'acquire' an ego until they are about three years old—or more specifically, the age at which they achieve genuine memory. From this it is reasonable to contend that egotists never grow up; they remain at the stage of babyhood, and in effect this is undeniably the case. To the extent that people are selfish they give themselves up to self-love, and may well be skilled in the practice of manipulating others, even family and friends, to their own advantage, often in the most subtle and seemingly guileless ways. Strangely enough, such people might well be shocked when confronted by the realities of their behaviour. They may consider, consciously or unconsciously, that they somehow 'deserve' such privileges and benefits, and have rights to them which are reasonable and justifiable.

At the opposite end of the spectrum are of course the true altruists, those who hold dear not so much their own interests, but rather those of others. We can all appreciate the merits involved in loving our neighbours as ourselves, at least theoretically, and indeed may well make generous gestures accordingly, particularly when urged to do so by a healthy conscience. Furthermore, there is more virtue in loving those who hate us than those who love us, for exchanging mutual affection involves much that is pleasurable and gratifying, and is effortless anyway. Of course we are all guilty of egotistical behaviour, but it is always a healthy sign when we feel that we should subordinate our interests to those of others as often as we can, even if it does hurt a little. Further reflection along these lines will bring the realization that the more we give ourselves up to self-love the more barren we become in our inner life.

If this becomes the case it may be to our advantage, for then the *cosmic law of self-correction* begins to work. Rudolf Steiner asserted that whenever egotism in individuals takes a wrong turn, the time comes when they become aware of its powers of self-annihilation, and eventually realize that altruism brings its own rewards.[8] As the ego grows stronger and more conscious of this fact, so will its powers of self-denial and self-subordination be deployed in favour of other members of society whenever valid opportunities to do so present themselves.

If the ego is weak, it expresses itself in egotism and self-centredness, and in autocratic behaviour. We all know that a bully is at heart a coward, and that an arrogant, domineering person lacks the inner firmness and assurance of someone who acts with courage and quiet deliberation. We all experience the struggle between our higher nature represented by our true ego, which is capable of self-sacrifice, modesty and humility, and our lower nature with its selfish, often hedonistic desires and its urge to manipulate the environment for egotistical reasons—of which we may or may not be fully conscious. We would do well to strive towards such self-consciousness, for this would require the development of a healthy conscience—an important demand of our times.

A word of warning

It is the duty of us all to be careful not to inflict our own temperament on others. Rudolf Steiner gave examples of excessively choleric behaviour on the part of parents and teachers who frighten and shock children during their early years, perhaps unwittingly. Such behaviour may well result in digestive and other metabolic disorders in adulthood. Similarly, the moods and actions of a parent, teacher or significant other whose temperament is extraordinarily melancholic may so affect the children that their life of feeling is 'chilled', and such constraints placed upon their inner life could cause irregularities of breathing and blood-circulation, heart trouble and allied complaints to occur in later life.

Again, a phlegmatic teacher whose basic indifference inhibits free exchange of thoughts and feelings with the pupils may induce nervous disorders when they are older. Lack of firm direction and guidance from an excessively sanguine adult may result in children suffering later on from listlessness and lack of vitality and zest for life, as well as lack of will-power and perseverance in face of difficulties.[9]

However, it certainly is possible for us to change our main and subsidiary temperaments consciously and deliberately, difficult though this may be. To do so obviously calls not only for a strong ego but also for thorough self-knowledge, particularly with regard to temperamental traits. Rudolf Steiner certainly gave plenty of advice concerning self-development, particularly in his books *How to Know Higher Worlds* and *Occult Science,* and must have the last word in this regard:

> Through wise self-knowledge it is possible, in the course of esoteric development, to repair the damage done by the predominant temperament. One begins to feel convinced that this damage can be repaired by bringing about modifications with the other temperaments; one must be aware of the effect of the transformations in relation to the other temperaments.[10]

Chapter 3

An Artistic View of the World

> It is only when, by starting from an intellectual understanding we are able to pass over to an artistic understanding, and then develop this artistic understanding into a principle of knowledge, that we can discover what lives within us in a human way, and not in accordance with the ways of nature out there in the macrocosm. We then find the relationship between humankind and the universe in a true sense.[1]

Art and science are mutually supportive

Because our temperaments blend into our whole individuality, our character defies exact quantification in rigid scientific terms. Just as we ourselves are continually active in our emotional and intellectual natures, any one moment can give only a snapshot, a single frame in a very long film. The art of living really is an art, and we call upon ourselves to be constantly busy at practising it. At the same time we must observe the rules obtaining in the science of living, for it makes sense to bear in mind the maxim that what's good for the beehive is good for the bee.

Certainly, it is always to our advantage if we can loosen up our thinking, get rid of any prejudices, and open up our minds to new ideas and fresh ways of looking at things, and much of this chapter concerns the value of this practice. A lively imagination is always a great asset if it is not allowed to run away with us. Willing suspension of disbelief is also of great benefit. Reserving judgement until cases have been as thoroughly examined as possible should be the rule, needless to say, and the advantages of possessing an enquiring mind are obvious. Close observation and attention to detail should come as standard, as should the search for every possible symptom relevant to whatever the case may be, and the facts be allowed to speak for themselves. But however coldly objective we might strive to be, we can never claim to view things without a certain degree of subjectivity. We cannot entirely escape either the conditioning and indoctrination acquired in our early childhood years, or the fact that wherever we turn our gaze in the universe we see that of which we are truly part.

The whole matter of viewing oneself within the universe from a standpoint of self and not-self, as subject and object, can lead us into the realms of philosophy, but such an exercise is well worth the effort involved. Rudolf Steiner put the whole matter in a nutshell when he wrote:

> The cognitive faculty appears to human beings as subjective only so long as he does not notice that it is nature itself who speaks through this faculty. Subjective and objective meet when the objective world of ideas lives in the subject and when all that is active in nature itself lives in the human spirit. When this happens, all antithesis between subject and object ceases.[2]

If this approach should be too daunting, it might be easier for you to accompany in imagination the oriental sage when he takes his pupil to the top of the mountain and, with a wide sweep of his arm, makes the pronouncement, 'Thou art that.' At an appropriate time later he repeats the situation, but this time declaring, 'That art thou.' Any comment from me concerning such scenarios might well be superfluous, and may even spoil your own efforts, but many people have found this exercise very productive.

When it first dawns on us that there is, in the final

analysis, no essential difference between the subjective and the objective, it ranks as a real achievement. We are so inextricably bound up with the whole cosmos in far more ways we do not know about than ways we do, and we should foster every urge to *trust* it, and take every opportunity not only to gain confidence in the universe but also to gain confidence in ourselves and our newly enlivened thinking.

Medieval thinkers were influenced by the so-called 'doctrine of signatures', which held that the shape or form of certain natural objects or phenomena gave clues as to their nature or function—a kind of 'reading the book of Nature'. For example, the likeness of the eye to the flower of the plant Eyebright (*Euphrasia*) suggested to physicians of those times that it could be useful for treating eye disorders, and such medicaments are to be found on chemists' shelves today. Again, ancient physicians prescribed beetroot for blood disorders simply because of its rich red colour, in their eyes reminiscent of blood, and this notion is not without foundation, for 'beetroot has the ability to strengthen and cool the blood, promoting a clear and pink skin and has a mildly tonic effect on the heart.'[3]

This kind of approach is now widely regarded as simplistic or naïve, but the underlying principles are still with us in various forms, despite the fact that it smacks of 'sympathetic magic'. We still refer to storm-clouds and rough seas as being 'angry' or 'threatening', and the notion of the 'language of flowers' is with us yet. However, we may be able to make use of such ideas when attempting to 'read' the characteristic properties and conditions involving both ourselves and outer nature. The archetypal qualities of Fire, Air, Water and Earth are certainly useful in this respect, and we would be unwise to dismiss the whole doctrine of signatures out of hand, for it is often possible to descry the workings of archetypal principles and forces in their modes of manifestation, and 'read' their messages which are there for all who have eyes to see.

For example, with regard to these four elements—just imagine—they are clearly discernible in the placing or siting of the natural 'elements' themselves. Earth is of course the lowest, upon which rests the waters in various guises, above which is water vapour, borne by the Air, the whole being warmed through by Fire, and heat always rises! So we have a living picture of the two gravitational elements (Earth and Water) and the two levitational elements (Air and Fire). Furthermore, if we take them in order from the highest to the lowest, we have a faithful picture of the Earth's evolutionary stages from the heat of Old Saturn, through the airy nature of Old Sun and the watery nature of Old Moon to the solid earth now beneath our feet.

The four elements are demonstrably truly archetypal in nature, faithfully reminiscent as they are of the four stages of evolution that we, and indeed our planet itself, have undergone to date, as touched on also in Chapter 1. It should also be clear to any observer that Creation is divided into four clearly distinguishable realms, namely, the mineral, plant, animal and human kingdoms, all of which are closely and necessarily interconnected and interdependent. Nature discovered ecology long before we did, and the newly resurrected notion that the world in which we live actually carries on a life of its own, and is capable of regulating its diverse features and attributes, is becoming quite popular. However, this notion is still essentially mechanistic, for most of its proponents do not really believe that our planetary home Gaea or Gaia, now commonly so called after the Greek goddess of the Earth, is a living being—but it is.

Interesting in itself is the way we commonly speak of the

activities which are going on under and above us as well as around us in the whole of Nature, and which are beyond our control. We allude to it as *it* rather than 'she' unthinkingly, employing this pronoun in familiarly casual fashion without even bothering to consider what, if any, antecedent noun it refers to. We say *'it'* is cloudy, raining, snowing, freezing, foggy, windy or whatever, rarely stopping to ponder precisely what this 'it' is. Contemplating on such usage can be a profitable exercise, and I recommend it in the light of what follows.

An art of interpreting nature?

Johann Wolfgang von Goethe (1749–1832), the eminent German poet, dramatist, scientist and 'universal man', saw fit to express some of his scientific ideas in poetic form. To him the *idea* was all-important, and he was convinced that Nature proceeds according to idea in the same manner as all human beings follow an idea in all actions they undertake. In his work *The Metamorphosis of Plants*, he expresses his scientific ideas concerning the archetypal principle that the whole proceeds from its parts, in artistic style. The idea of our oneness with the Universal All was central to his thinking, and it is encouraging in this day and age to observe that people are again beginning to realize the truth of this, and really are taking ecology and our responsibilities towards the Earth seriously. Concerning Goethe and his work, the scholar D. Luke had this to say:

> It was Goethe's basic conviction, expressed both in his scientific and literary works, that man and nature are bound to each other by a profound correlation, that nature is a whole, that its processes are gradual and orderly, *that its laws are also those of human life and art.*[4] (My italics)

Goethe, as both artist and scientist, found it distressing that many of his contemporaries maintained that a person could not be both at the same time. Their view that the strict objectivity of science was bound to clash with the allegedly subjective nature of art within the same individual both puzzled and saddened him. He asserted that in artistic creation, that which appears in science as Idea is expressed as Image, whether represented in sense-perceptible objects or whether mentally perceptible. As reflection will show, whereas Science produces ideas from the world of Nature, Art makes use of various materials from this world in order to clothe its Ideas. That Rudolf Steiner heartily agreed with Goethe is made plain:

> So long as Man has no sense of the working of the creative activity of the idea, his thinking is divorced from living Nature. He must regard thinking as a purely subjective activity that is able to project an abstract picture of nature. But directly he senses the way in which the idea lives and is active in his inner being he regards himself and Nature as one Whole, and what makes its appearance in his inner being as a subjective element is for him at the same time objective; he knows that he no longer confronts Nature as a stranger, but he feels that he has grown together with the whole of her. The subjective has become the objective; the objective is wholly permeated with the spirit.[5]

More and more people are coming to the realization that we are *of* the universe as well as *in* it, but all too often this notion still tends to remain as an abstraction. The most likely reason for this is that orthodox educational thinking is thoroughly intellectualistic and therefore thoroughly materialistic. Nature is all too often reduced to sets of laws which take in the various scientific disciplines, there being little attempt to view the world as a gigantic work of art.

There also seems to be a reluctance, at once unreasonable and unfortunate, to search for examples that would serve to support this view.

Orthodox thinking maintains for the most part that form in the natural world is influenced by scientific rather than artistic factors. This reluctance is all the more irrational in view of the immense store of traditional wisdom which points unmistakably in the direction of nature as manifesting artistic as well as scientific principles. God is undeniably a mathematician, but He is also a superb artist. Merely because many of these uncluttered pre-scientific notions appear simplistic, and perhaps too vague and generalized, does not necessarily indicate that they are lacking in scientific validity.

Our will to know and to understand represents demands of human nature; objects surrounding us can impart to us no more of their nature and being than we are able to exact from them. In this respect, therefore, and from this point of view, it is nonsense to speak of boundaries of knowledge, of limits to our cognitive faculties. The key to the matter lies in the strength of the demands we make in order to extend our cognition and comprehension of nature; there are no boundaries except those which we ourselves put up. Rudolf Steiner repeatedly asserted that nature and humanity must not be studied merely according to logic, but according to a reasoning acquired only when intellectual perception has passed over into artistic perception.

General principles of two-, three- and fourfolding

The archetypal pattern of fourfolding is as important and significant as that of threefolding. In many respects they run parallel to each other, and quite often it is possible to

An Artistic View of the World 45

discern that on numerous occasions a fourfold model is a slightly modified threefold one in disguise, and that 4 into 3 really will 'go' without resorting to too much in the way of trickery![6] A typical example of this is encountered in reconciling our threefold nature (spirit, soul, body) with our fourfold nature (ego, astral, etheric and physical bodies), of which more anon.

Just as God will not be mocked, Nature will not be fooled. A model that is even more primal than threefolding is that of *polarity*, that is to say, when two factors in nature are opposite to each other and contrary in every respect. A common and fitting example of this is the spirit-matter polarity, as exemplified in our own constitution of spirit and body. But whenever a polarity arises, a field of tension or interaction comes into existence between the two sets of opposing forces, qualities, characteristics, attributes or whatever. Thus something new is created: the twofold gives rise to the threefold; the duality is transformed into a trichotomy. Where the spirit-body polarity in human beings is concerned, it is the *soul* which is created, a process which was so neatly expressed by Irenaeus (*c.* 130–*c.* 200), a Church Father, in his treatise *Against Heresies* as follows:

> The perfect person consists of these three: flesh, soul and Spirit. One of these saves and fashions—that is, the spirit. Another is united and formed—that is, the flesh; while that which lies between the two is the soul, which sometimes follows the Spirit and is raised by it, but at other times sympathizes with the flesh and is drawn into it by earthly passions.

As we shall see, the pivotal position occupied by the third (secondary and central and/or pivotal) factor which comes into existence between two factors that are in polar opposition to each other is of the greatest significance; indeed, it is how most threefold models are formulated. An example of two sets of polarities which are archetypal in nature and whose characteristics carry many connotations both physical and soul-spiritual are the primary conditions of Cold and Warm, and Wet and Dry—an obviously fourfold arrangement:

Cold

Wet   Dry

Warm

It is worth repeating at this point that the insistence upon cold, proven facts characteristic of orthodox science scarcely applies where issues of an archetypal nature are involved, for these are at once all-encompassing and multi-faceted, and are applicable in general rather than particular terms. The methodologies which are incorporated into the practices of modern science are disposed towards specialism and hence fragmentation. This tendency implies an overall inclination to proceed from the parts to the whole, whereas the principles of Rudolf Steiner's spiritual science are in line with the method advocated and indeed practised by Goethe, namely, that of proceeding from the whole to its parts.

According to ancient Greek thinking, the natural world consists of four elements, namely, Fire, Air, Water and Earth, and various admixtures of these, and which without stretching reality and our imagination too far can also be understood as two sets of polarities: Fire and Water, and Air and Earth. Again, with the employment of not too much in the way of imagination, we can add these four to our original model, thus:

```
              Cold
      Water        Earth
  Wet                   Dry
      Air          Fire
              Warm
```

All this seems reasonable enough, and only brief indications are sufficient to stir our imagination. We know that Earth carries the attributes of coldness and dryness, and it is easy to deduce that, in terms of temperament, this conformation comes most closely to the dry, bony nature of the melancholic. Obviously, Water is cold and wet, and the very word phlegmatic is enough to arouse direct understanding of the ponderous, oceanic nature of those who can be described by it, living as they do in their glandular system and their body fluids. Our own breath, moist and warm as it is, typifies the element of the Air and the sanguine temperament—variable, capricious and refreshing. Fire is nothing but hot and dry, and the enthusiasm, energy and the generally unquenchable nature of the typical choleric person comes to mind. It is therefore quite easy to allocate the appropriate positions of the four temperaments to our earlier model, arriving at one that is equally elegant and valid:

```
                    Cold
   PHLEGMATIC        MELANCHOLIC
           Water        Earth
    Wet                      Dry
            Air        Fire
    SANGUINE           CHOLERIC
                    Warm
```

An archetypal model of our constitution

The threefold arrangement is mirrored in our physiological make-up, in that body, soul and spirit are represented by the head (brain and nerves-senses system), the rhythmic system (heart and lungs), and the metabolic-limbs system, as will be shown directly. However, it is correct as well as more appropriate for present purposes to regard our whole constitution as being fourfold, especially so because they so nicely match the four temperaments. If we take the spirit-body polarity, we can again split these two into two more, which necessarily take on the polaric nature of the original pairing — in other words, into our soul-spiritual nature (ego and astral body), and corporeal nature (physical body and etheric or life-body).

The Bible and the scriptural writings of other religions and traditions, and also myths and legends, frequently provide pointers and clues as to the nature of ourselves and the world we inhabit. These references to certain images, descriptions of imaginations and so on are of course not arbitrary, but individuals must make of them what they can or will. In Ezekiel 1:5 we read: *And out of the midst (of the fire) came the likeness of four living creatures. And this was their appearance; they had the likeness of a man.*

This description is further amplified in verse 10 of the same chapter: *As for the likeness of their faces, they four had the face of a man, and the face of a lion, on the right side; and they four had the face of an ox on the left side; they four also had the face of an eagle.* The theme is taken up in the New Testament in Revelation 4:7: *And the first beast was like a lion, and the second beast like a calf, and the third beast had a face as a man, and the fourth beast was like a flying eagle.*

These four creatures also occur in traditional astrology, in that they represent the four Elements and 'fixed' signs of the zodiac as follows: Air = Aquarius or Water-bearer as a human being, often winged and reminiscent of the traditional concept of an angel; Earth = Taurus or Bull, calf or ox; Fire = Leo or Lion; and Water = Scorpio, or Scorpion, and also Eagle.[7] They also appear in artistic form in many churches and cathedrals, being associated with the four evangelists, namely, Aquarius with Matthew, Taurus with Mark, Leo with Luke, and Scorpio (as Eagle) with John. Worth noting too in these respects is the Sphinx of Ancient Egypt, with its human head, body of a bull, feet of a lion and wings of an eagle.

We can see therefore how deeply ingrained in our culture these four symbolic creatures are. An imaginative-artistic representation of the human being in this manner was made by Rudolf Steiner in his course of lectures *Man as Symphony of the Creative Word* as Eagle (head), Lion (rhythmic system) and Cow (metabolic system). He asserted on many occasions that the human being is representative of a synthesis of these three creatures, and symbolically as the crown of Creation itself. As an imagination, this portrayal of our constitution provides a rich source of material for contemplation and meditation.

How the threefold becomes the fourfold

The notion of ourselves as fourfold beings becoming reconciled with this threefold model—which is also virtually a fourfold model—is a fruitful one. If we take the basic threefold pattern of our whole constitution into consideration with particular reference to the four temperaments as personified in the four somatotypes, we find that in this case we can establish that four into three will actually 'go', physiologically if not mathematically. The underlying principle seems to be that the central element which arises within and occupies the field of operation between two poles, itself shows propensities to lean or incline towards either of these two poles.

Hence in effect this central factor becomes itself threefold, and a good example of this general rule is seen in the two opposing soul-elements of antipathy and sympathy which show inclinations respectively towards thinking and willing. At the same time, this arrangement facilitates the original threefold model to be verifiably metamorphosed into a fourfold one, thus:

Spirit	Thinking (spiritual activity)	Truth	Waking
	Antipathy	Reason (spiritual)	
Soul	Feeling as ⟨ thinking in reserve / willing in reserve	Beauty	Dreaming
	Sympathy	Form (material)	
Body	Willing (bodily activity)	Goodness	Sleeping

The same principle can be seen to operate in the case of Truth, Beauty and Goodness, as the model shows. Beauty expresses that which is *true*, therefore involving the spirit, and also that which is *good*, which must be made manifest in and through matter by means of bodily (limbs) activity. The interconnections involving states of consciousness as shown are self-evident, and altogether valid.

The following model progresses from a simple twofold arrangement representative of our soul-spiritual, subjective, inner nature and our corporeal, objective, outer nature to more complex threefold and fourfold arrays. However, matters are never simple, and it must be noted that it is possible to subject it to a 'reversal' process, one which is commonly appropriate in the case of certain

An Artistic View of the World 51

similar models, in which the first (upper) and third (lower) factors are in polar opposition. What always remains constant is the central (second) factor, and the interchangeability of these polar opposites is readily seen to be legitimate.

Nature	Member	Principle	System	Creature	Element	Temperament
Soul spiritual	Spirit	Ego	Head-nerve	Eagle	Fire	Choleric
	Soul	Astral	Lungs ⎫ Rhythmic ⎬ Heart ⎭	Lion	Air Water	Sanguine Phlegmatic
Corporeal	Body	⎧ Etheric ⎩ Physical	Metabolic	Cow	Earth	Melancholic

Here we have constructed, at the same time, a model that is at once a unity, a duality and a trichotomy. In effect, we have a new principle that is at the same time three in one and one in three. Now this is precisely what we have in the particular model of eagle, lion and cow as elemental factors representative of a single human being comprising head-nerves system, rhythmic heart-lungs system, and metabolic-limbs system, all of which have a dual character. As we have consistently seen, the central zone is also twofold, arising as it does—indeed must do—between the polarities 'above' and 'below' it. It therefore constitutes an area of interaction between the two opposing elements. Thus the influences are reciprocal, proceeding to and from both factors which appear above and below it as a kind of tension field set up between them.

With these two dualities we arrive at a genuine fourfolding as well. For instance, the soul as pivotal central zone between the poles of spirit and body radiates its influences respectively as antipathy and sympathy. In similar fashion the rhythmic system, represented by the Lion, manifests as the lungs, whose function engages the element of Air, in the form of oxygen and carbon dioxide, and thereby also the heart, which employs the warm blood, that 'very special fluid', to carry these 'airy' elements as well as nutrients extracted from our food via the metabolic system, and whose distributary role is vital in serving our whole organism.

It should be clear from this that we are considering the sanguine (Air) and phlegmatic (Water) temperaments respectively. However, matters are not so simple, for we must consider that the choleric temperament has as much to do with willing as the melancholic has to do with thinking. Here we have the kind of paradox we often meet with when delving deeper into the various symptoms associated with all phenomena, and is a typical example of the principle of reversal which sometimes operates, and which serves as a warning not to apply the rigidities of intellectual logic, but rather to look at the whole matter artistically and to watch out for *apparent* contradictions.

This table well repays study and reflection. It is very reliable, and when, as we routinely check the solution to an arithmetical subtraction exercise by 'adding back' the answer to the subtrahend (the number which is to be subtracted) which should prove to be equal to the minuend (the number from which another is to be subtracted), so it is possible to gain in confidence by practising the art of thinking concretely. You will see at once that the upper two temperaments are subjective and the lower pair objective; and that our subjective nature is based in our soul-spiritual temperamental attributes whereas our objective nature is rooted in our corporeal organization. By quick reference to the preceding table, it is clear that the lungs levitate to our airy (mental) and spiritual (dynamic and driving) temperamental types, whereas our vascular system gravitates towards the corporeal (static and driven) temperamental categories.

Another example that is useful for meditative work, and perhaps even more so because the principle of reversal is also evident, is the likeness in constitution between the human being and the archetypal plant. That is to say, that when we imagine a plant as inverted, with the roots above and the flowering and fruiting parts below, connected of course by the stem-leaves structure, then, averred Steiner, it is truly representative of the human form and structure. The roots are then positioned as our head, the fruiting members correspond with our metabolic system as polar opposites, and the middle arrangement of stem with its offshoots with their leaves, often positioned in regular order, are a true comparison with our rhythmic system.

This is commonly regarded as a threefold organization, but as is so often the case the middle structure is itself twofold, perhaps also manifesting as opposing factors. What could be more contrary than the tubular structure of the stem, trunk, branches and twigs when compared with the flat, two-dimensional leaves? As we have seen, just as our soul-organization features the opposing factors of antipathy and sympathy, so we have in our bodily rhythmic system those of the lungs (air) and blood (water), the first having to do with the outer world and the second with the innermost reaches of the human body. It is no coincidence that in many cases both offshoots from the main stem and/or the leaves are arranged in rhythmical fashion. Interestingly enough, Rudolf Steiner asserted that with regard to nutrition, root crops affect our head-system, fruits of all kinds influence our metabolic-limbs system, and, needless to say perhaps, leafy vegetables are good for our rhythmic system of heart and lungs.

So there we have the fourfold archetypal plant which fits

our temperaments quite neatly and convincingly. The roots, hard, earthy and dark, are certainly reminiscent of melancholic characteristics. The stem, trunk and branches carry the 'life-blood' of the plant or tree in the form of sap, and are hence suggestive of the fluid-producing glands of the etheric body and therefore the inwardly orientated phlegmatic temperament. The leaves, perfectly adapted, in their flat, platelike form for taking in oxygen, carbon dioxide, nitrogen and other airy substances, are undeniably redolent of light, fluttering, outwardly orientated sanguine attributes and qualities. All fruits, from hard grains to soft berries, form and ripen under the influence of the sun's heat, and the warmth, enthusiasm and drive of the upward and outward striving choleric is brought to mind. Here again we have themes that can form a fruitful basis for further contemplation, and are recommended. This model of the fourfold plant is thus seen to be genuinely archetypal, and fully consistent with the traditional notion of the doctrine of signatures.

Again, we are not surprised when we learn that there are also four ethers, but lack of space forbids discussion of them here.[8] They are: warmth-ether, light-ether, sound-ether and life-ether, and are closely involved in the work of the elemental beings, of which, predictably, there are four categories. The gnomes are connected with the element of Earth; undines with that of Water; sylphs (fairies) with that of Air, and salamanders (fire-beings) with that of Fire.[9]

Again, discussion of these beings and their activities is not possible here, and the whole topic should be studied direct from Rudolf Steiner's own words, notably in this connection his inspiring *Man as Symphony of the Creative Word*. With all these foursomes we should not neglect the four seasons, the four kingdoms of nature, the four elements and so on, which also furnish plenty of issues for meditation.[10] Here is some relevant advice from Rudolf Steiner:

> Seek in your own being
> And you will find the world;
> Seek in the world-wide being
> And you will find yourself.
> Mark the constant swing
> Between self and world
> And you will find revealed:
> The human-cosmic-being,
> The cosmic-human-being.[11]

Chapter 4

A Meditative Approach to Self-knowledge

> In the boundless Without
> Find thyself, O Man!
>
> In the innermost Within
> Feel the boundless Worlds!
>
> So will it be revealed:
> Nowhere the Riddle of Worlds is solved,
> Save in the being of Man.[1]

Meet Lucifer and Ahriman

It will almost certainly be to your advantage if you come to some understanding concerning Lucifer and Ahriman. You will assuredly know these two by their common names — the Devil and Satan respectively. Nowadays scholars and others tend not to differentiate between these two, either lumping them together into one being or using both names interchangeably to refer to only one entity. There is some justification for doing this, and confusion has arisen because the Greek word *diabolos* does not of course appear in the Hebrew Old Testament. However, the case in favour of differentiation is very strong. Many people would be inclined to refer to the Bible to settle any misunderstanding, and there is evidence in the New Testament of two words being employed to personify the Tempter and the Evil One as two different beings. However, it must be said that some confusion does surround this problem of the Devil and Satan as duality or unity.

Both Matthew and John differentiate between two personified sources of affliction which work on us from out of the invisible worlds of spirit. In Matthew 4:1–7 it is the Devil (*diabolos*, false accuser) who tempts Christ Jesus in the wilderness; and the same word is used in Luke 8:12, John 8:44 and many other places. In Revelation 12:9 both the Devil and (the) Satan (Hebrew—*Satana*, adversary) are mentioned in the same verse, as they are in Matthew 12:26 and Revelation 20:2. Matthew calls Beelzebub 'the prince of devils', and clearly identifies him with Satan (Matthew 12:24–27). Mark echoes this (3:22,23), as does Luke (3:18,19). Further clues are provided by the so-called Lord's Prayer, whereby entreaty is made to 'lead us not into temptation, but deliver us from evil' (Matthew 6:13), thereby suggesting that the powers responsible for so testing us are separate entities rather than the same one. It is therefore a matter for individual investigation and decision.

The Devil is the Tempter, and it is he and his minions who 'promise the Earth', who inspire enthusiasm and ardour, and fascination, enchantment and enticement, usually in that order. By these devices they tempt us to go just that little bit too far—and into trouble. Satan is the Evil One, who with his demonic assistants seeks to entrap and beguile us by employing lies, half-truths, and deceitful wiles of every kind. Whereas Lucifer would whirl us away into the very heavens themselves, Ahriman fosters our self-interest, and by cold but suspect logic would bind us fast in matter and turn us into automatons, sclerotic in body and rigidly set in mind. So by long tradition we have two tor-mentors who were sent by God to enable us to become perfect, even as He is perfect. On our left we have the Devil, also known as Lucifer, and on our right is Ahriman, also known as Satan.[2]

Lucifer (Latin—light-bearer) and Ahriman (Persian—*anri mainya*, the evil spirit) are, strictly speaking, collective nouns employed for all spiritual beings of diabolic or satanic nature who do the mischief as far as human beings are concerned. It may be helpful, in attempting to discern which influences are active, and how and where they are at work, to ponder the fact that Ahriman, in Zoroastrian times, was regarded as the spirit of darkness (and by inference, of evil), whose antagonist was Ahura Mazda, as representative of light and goodness. However, Lucifer must not be identified with Ahura Mazda, but regarded as possessing some of his qualities.[3]

Ahriman is the master of *delusion*, whereby we become subject to falsehoods and misapprehensions of every kind, and our perception of reality, particularly *inner* reality, becomes warped and unreliable. Beelzebub or Mephistopheles, as Goethe confirms, is the 'father of lies', and is generally of a negative nature—the spirit that denies. However, no entity can be entirely negative in the absolute sense, for as Mephistopheles himself recognizes, he is 'Part of that Power, not understood, Which always wills the Bad, and always works the Good'.[4] Moreover, it is easy to understand that, as Steiner pointed out, Ahriman is the god of hindrance, disease and death. Self-delusion all too easily paves the way to pessimism and dark moods, melancholy and self-absorption, during which time it is difficult for the sufferer to make decisions which may generate a swing away from depression and apathy to optimism and action.

Lucifer, on the other hand, is the master of *illusion*, by which we become induced to perceive what is imaginary or non-existent in the *outer* world. Our feet do not, so to speak, touch the ground, and we tend to become engrossed in the realm of daydreams and exaggerated expectations, unrealistic hopes, wishes and desires, and over-optimistic attitudes generally. Strength and energy are squandered in fatuous, nebulous and trifling initiatives and activities of all kinds in efforts to catch tenuous and illusive 'shifting shapes'.

Characterizations such as these are entirely representative of the influences of Lucifer and Ahriman, and Rudolf Steiner went as far as to contend that in the course of time the validity of the meanings behind the proper adjectives Luciferic and Ahrimanic would be acknowledged, and correctly and usefully employed.

It can be readily discerned that the attributes and qualities listed earlier are for the most part in polar opposition. It is as though we constitute a kind of battlefield upon which Lucifer and Ahriman wage war in which we human beings are the prize. Whatever else, we can also detect that in order to maintain our essential humanity we must tread a middle way between the two sets of powers. In the field of interaction between Lucifer and Ahriman it is to be expected that individuals find themselves attracted to one or the other in varying degrees of intensity from time to time.

Most of us have been taught that the Devil, Satan, Beelzebub and their like are our enemies. But if we take the earlier quotation from Goethe's *Faust* seriously and ponder it well, we see that Goethe was justified in saying this. We would be prudent also to take equally seriously what Rudolf Steiner said concerning them, for here is wisdom: 'The acts of supersensible beings can be described as good or bad; the beings themselves—never!'[5] With these notions in mind, it might be helpful if we take time to ponder the consequences of the actions of us human beings on the members of the animal, plant, and indeed the mineral kingdoms. Do we act evilly when we deliberately influence and perhaps modify the life and being of animals and plants in the name of perfection—only to eat them afterwards? Such an example may be regarded as somewhat tasteless, but it is serious too, and the comparison is sound.

The Jester speaks

In my Preface I touched lightly on the connections between the four suits of playing cards and our four temperaments, hinting that the notion may not be a matter of mere coincidence. There is always a Joker in the pack, of course, and his facetious observations and remarks should be taken for the brazen exaggerations they are. There are many interpretations of the symbols appearing on the cards, and this is merely another. The Luciferic suits appear in red as hearts and diamonds, as appropriate to the two active temperaments, namely, choleric and sanguine. The Ahrimanic suits, namely clubs and spades, appear in heavy, sombre black as a colour that generally befits their murky peculiarities.

This Joker ventures to suggest that sanguines be associated with the flickering red hearts as characteristic of their fickle waywardness, swinging from sympathy to antipathy and back again with effortless rapidity. They are recurrently involved in actual affairs of the heart (for they are great charmers), and may well eventually find themselves knee-deep in broken hearts, resting among which would probably be a few replicas of their own. Red diamonds are entirely appropriate to cholerics, with their inflamed egos, sharp corners and all too often heartless ambitions. In their will to succeed they are demonstrating for all to see their conviction that diamonds are the only friends to be trusted.

As for their dark and often complex and inscrutable opposite numbers, the spades and clubs seem to him as representing respectively the dull and heavy phlegmatics and the incessantly aggressive melancholics. The former feel secure only when they have dug themselves well and truly in against every attack or even disturbance. The latter are never happier in their misery than when they are bludgeoning either their long-suffering associates or themselves, or whosoever dares to bring a little light, however faintly showing, into their benighted lives, and balm for their diverse complaints.

Lucifer and Ahriman do not have the faintest clue as to what balancing out means, and so we have to do it all ourselves. Although we may not realize it, we are engaged in a constant battle for balance between the opposing influences of Lucifer and Ahriman, and we can be sure that this arrangement is part of a grand cosmic plan by which we are enabled to advance on the road to perfection, slowly but surely. We will come to realize that this is indeed the case, and that instead of by mere chance human nature is what it is on account of powers decidedly more mighty than we.

But our disappointments, fears, misgivings and other negative traits tend to disappear when we stoically accept our plight, for as there are hierarchies ranged above us, so there are those ranked below us, namely, the animal, plant and mineral kingdoms, which all have their destinies to meet. Even the gods themselves are in process of evolving, for nothing remains static; they and we must needs either progress or retrogress, and the only sensible path to take is that which leads us upwards and on.

We may safely trust the Universe

Feelings of being in union with God, or of being identified with the Universe, are common enough even among ordinary men and women from time to time, but these are for the most part rarely spoken about, either out of modesty or fear of ridicule. This sense of oneness with Creation is nicely put by the famous thirteenth-century Sufi mystic and poet Jalalu'l-din Rumi as follows:

> I died as mineral and became a plant;
> I died as plant and rose to animal;
> I died as animal and I was Man.
> Why should I fear? When was I less by dying?
> Yet once more I shall die as a Man, to soar
> With angels blest; but even from angelhood
> I must pass on...

He saw human progress through a series of *stages* rather than actual *states*, and presents in a few words a picture much grander than that which modern science does. He connects himself with the mineral world inasmuch as his physical body is composed of it; he relates himself to the plant world in so far as he grows, propagates his species and perishes; and at the animal stage he perceives, by means of sense-organs, his environment, but reacts to the impressions gained from it merely at an instinctual level. But as a man he experience *self*-consciousness by virtue of possessing a feeling of genuine selfhood, which animals lack. The next stage in evolution is that of the angelic, but even this condition cannot, for him, mark the end of his path to perfection, which he sees as ascending to God Himself, who alone is perfect.

With regard to these matters many people acknowledge that there is a certain inevitability about the Hermetic axiom 'As above, so below; as below, so above', for the indications for its validity are many and diverse. A similar notion echoing this notion was stated by Rudolf Steiner in meditative form:

> Throughout the wide world there lives and moves
> The real Being of Man.

A Meditative Approach to Self-knowledge   63

While in the innermost core of Man
The mirror-image of the World is living.

The 'I' unites the two,
And thus fulfils
The meaning of existence.[6]

So we may justifiably have confidence in the Universe; and in any case we are part of it, a veritable microcosm within the macrocosm, as Steiner's illuminating verse describes. We share it with myriads of other spiritual beings, some more advanced than we, and some less so, and although we may not be aware of it whilst constrained by our Earthly consciousness, we mingle with them as they do with us. This has always been known, of course. In Paul's Letters to the Ephesians, Colossians and Galatians, spiritual hierarchies such as Authorities, Principalities, Powers, Mights (which also bear various other names in different versions of the New Testament) are all mentioned. However, they are commonly — but mistakenly — regarded as representing civil governmental authorities. Cherubim, Seraphim and Thrones are also mentioned, but these are widely thought of in vague terms of unclassified 'heavenly hosts' rather than what they actually are, namely, exalted spiritual beings of the highest hierarchy. More familiar to most people are Angels and Archangels who rank immediately above ourselves, and indeed are widely acknowledged in some form or other.

We have as special a relationship to the 'fallen angels' Lucifer and Ahriman and their hordes of helpers as they have to us, and this in very intimate ways.[7] We are not conscious of them as such, but rather of their influences on us, and these are for the most part those listed earlier on, all of which are easily recognizable as being of a soul-spiritual nature. Thus, in terms of our four temperaments we are able to perceive that the choleric and sanguine pair are affected directly by Lucifer, the bearer of the light and warmth of consciousness itself, whereas the phlegmatic and melancholic duo are influenced more by Ahriman, that dark and cold spirit who belongs to the subterranean realms.

Any serious attempt we make to smooth out our temperaments must involve earnest efforts in the way of self-knowledge. This is in any case desirable for it has the important advantage of learning about those of our friends and neighbours, workmates and playmates as well. Even more consequential is the fact that we shall be called upon to even out our sympathies and antipathies during our sojourn in the soul-world after death—and that's the hard way.[8]

The first step is of course to determine our own main and secondary temperaments, and pay attention to the various circumstances in which they make themselves felt, and the nature of the regularities and irregularities involved. We should take note as to when seemingly spontaneous or hesitant reactions result in certain modes of behaviour on our part. Responses may come under the *always, not always, hardly ever* or *never* heading, and tendencies to *act out of character* should be carefully noted and steps taken to modify our reactions accordingly. Most people consider themselves far from perfect, and this is a healthy attitude. Furthermore, most people harbour the wish, if not intention, to leave the world a better place than they found it, and efforts to this end are more likely to be successful when a fair working knowledge of the temperaments is acquired.

Living into our surroundings

The general conditions of our home and its surroundings often have profound effects on us. It is of far-reaching importance whether we as children lived in a high-rise flat or a hill farm, whether our home setting was agreeably wholesome or not, and so on. Likewise, whether we work in a noisy factory, aboard ship, or in a lively classroom is also of great significance. Our many roles that we play during our passage through life, singly or simultaneously, all work back on us to a greater or lesser degree, and contribute to our overall disposition. In a very real sense the outer becomes the inner, just as our inner impulses help shape the outer, for we really do construct our own private world within the public world.

We have no choice but to live in—and live *into*—the four kingdoms of Nature to which we belong, and which are representative of the four Elements with their many correlations with the four temperaments. Experiencing the four seasons of the year, and the various festivals as they occur, is an obvious way in which we can become more involved in the cycle of each year as it passes. It is always most effective if this 'living into' can be achieved in contemplative, imaginative ways. We carry all four within us, and there is much in the outer world which is reflective of our own being and existence. In order not to impose myself in this respect, I have deliberately confined the observations and comments to a minimum, given as they are rather in the manner of hints which may be developed individually and according to personal experiences and predilections.[9]

The general notion of our 'living into' Nature is becoming more and more acknowledged for the reality that it is, as the growing public concern about ecological, environmental, and conservational matters, animal rights and so-called genetic engineering amply demonstrates. What we commonly recognize as 'human nature' equates roughly with what we acknowledge as the assortment of characteristics that distinguishes us from those by which the animal, plant and mineral kingdoms are represented. Curiously enough, though at the same not unexpectedly, our essential humanity can be seen to include these three lower orders, and with them their own salient qualities and attributes. Thus we have had incorporated into our very constitution many of these, in principle if not actually in detail.

The usual or customary manner in which we thus live into Nature is of great relevance and consequence in respect of both ourselves and our entire sensory as well as super-sensory environment, during both our life on the Earth and in the Heavenly realms after death. Such matters are complex, and for present purposes it is appropriate only to draw attention to them. For example, if we regard exceptionally attractive areas of outstanding natural beauty as mere 'beauty spots' to be merely and perhaps hurriedly gawped at before passing on to another and yet another in what soon becomes a tiresome succession, this can be detrimental to both our planet and ourselves.[10] However, if we take due regard for the spiritual aspects which are also necessarily involved, we can actually assist in the welfare not only of the elemental beings which inhabit the Earth and its phenomena and processes but hosts of other spiritual beings as well.[11]

Self-indulgence in the more sensory delights offered by nature as a whole can be contrasted with the erroneous notion that we would do better, so to speak, to contemplate our navel and confine ourselves to delving around in our own inner natures. Rudolf Steiner was insistent that 'world-knowledge is self-knowledge and self-knowledge is world knowledge':

> Knowledge proves fruitful upon the sole condition that it brings ourselves into harmony with the rest of the world. We must become one with the world if our knowledge is to

enliven us. It is for this reason that all knowledge which seeks the great truths of existence, selflessly and step by step, proves so helpful for the soul and consequently for the physical body. On the other hand we are brought into discord with the world through every form of solitary and purely self-centred brooding which severs our living connection with the world. Such things harden our soul and make us ill.[12]

In all this we do well to bear in mind, as he makes clear in the same lecture, that for everything which we can find in human beings there is something analogous which can be discovered in the rest of the world. Steiner gives useful examples of this principle and he was always careful to stress the moral aspects that accompany our interrelationships with the whole of Creation:

> In spiritual science we are seeking the thoughts of the gods wherewith they have guided the course of evolution ... and this ... creates in us a deep morality. Knowledge of spiritual science not only brings us wisdom consciously rather than instinctively, as formerly, but we receive a moral stimulus as well.[13]

Such indications serve us well when 'living into' our surroundings. When we observe the mineral, earthy world about us, with its contrasting contours, solid and resistant, personifying permanence and changelessness, scan its flat and monotonous plains and barren deserts with their air of purity and serenity, stand in awe of the majestic mountains that tower above us, remote, noble and immovable, and enjoy the sweet and comforting friendliness of gently rolling landscapes patterned with fields, woods and settlements, we feel part of it all — and so, of course, we are. All this is suggestive of our own feelings of ponderous earthiness which, however, requires much in the way of purpose and effort to overcome the all-pervading gravity, both physical and metaphysical in nature and implication.

The Watery element, by contrast to the Earthly, is rarely still, and any appearance of flat calm is deceptive, for invariably there is constant movement due to undercurrents, changes in temperature or other causes. This archetypal urge for all water itself and indeed all fluids to smooth out is seen in their main characteristic, namely, that of finding their own level. Inevitably, this implies a tendency towards inertia, literally a lack of self-motivation. The 'restless waves' and wavelets invariably display rhythms and counter-rhythms according to prevailing circumstances, and these may therefore be either *form-making* or *form-taking* in their effects. That is to say, when there exists little or no motion water has no option but to fill and hence take on the form of whatever contains or accommodates it; but when a considerable volume of water is forced into movement on account of external factors, such as changes in gradient (e.g. a waterfall) or by violent air disturbance as in storm conditions, it is capable of reshaping by force its own boundaries or limits, perhaps permanently.

Perhaps the main characteristic of Air is its uncertainty; ever unpredictable and wavering, 'blowing where it listeth', it is uncontrollable and unreliable. Never in any one place for long, like the birds, butterflies and other airborne creations it upholds, it passes through, passes by, passes on. As breeze and fair wind, blast or squall, draught or jet-stream, it is everywhere present, whether welcome or not. Moving air has an affinity with water, as with waves, but it also co-operates with it in its attenuated state, namely, as vaporous clouds, mist and fog, and even heavier particles such as snow, hail or raindrops, but sometimes also with tiny specks of earth, as in the case of smoke and dust-

A Meditative Approach to Self-knowledge 69

storms, and sometimes even with heavy material, as in the case of destructive gales and tornados. It has much to do with levity and very little with gravity, and perhaps this is why it is associated with being carefree, and all too often carelessness.

The element of Fire is not always easy to manage, and is well known as a good servant but a bad master. Its combustive activities come in many guises and cover a mighty range. Heat may well foster propagation and growth, but it can also bring death and destruction. Its polar opposite and greatest enemy in many respects is Water, but when they co-operate truly great deeds can be done. Air can be a close and co-operative partner and quite frequently its servant, albeit an unstable and untrustworthy one. Of all four elements, this is perhaps the most versatile and wide-ranging. In view of its wayward character it is the most difficult to handle, which must always be with care.

Reading the clouds

Rudolf Steiner often asserted that when we are confronted by a matter that requires investigation we should invariably adopt a phenomenological-symptomatological approach. In other words, we should in as full consciousness as possible observe, study and give our whole attention to, and bring our concentration to bear on, whatever facts are made available to us by these means. Propositions and theories should always come later, and be carefully and painstakingly constructed and applied.

In his book *Man or Matter*,[14] Goethean scientist Dr Ernst Lehrs did much to foster the great value of regarding the world artistically, and succeeds to a great extent in demonstrating that this procedure is just as valid as a strictly scientific approach. He discusses the work of

Goethe, Luke Howard (1772–1864) and John Ruskin (1819–1900), all of whom were 'true readers in the book of nature'. It is worth quoting one example of the work of both Goethe and Howard with regard to clouds and their forms. Interestingly enough, Howard, after many years of studying 'the countenance of the sky', identified four main types of cloud formation, naming and describing them as follows:

Cirrus: Parallel, flexuous or divergent fibres extensible in any and all directions.
Cumulus: Convex or conical heaps, increasing upwards from a horizontal base.
Stratus: A widely extended, continuous horizontal sheet, increasing from below.
Nimbus: The rain cloud.[15]

Modern meteorology identifies at least ten formations which, however, tend to disregard and at the same time blur the four archetypal formations and represent rather various intermediate conditions, for example the cirro-stratus, strato-cumulus and cumulo-nimbus configurations.

At first, any comparisons between these four cloud-formations and the four temperaments may seem fanciful at best, and at worst making the facts fit the assumption. No attempt is being made to 'prove' anything, of course. The main purpose of this discussion is to stimulate individual thinking-imagination, and to give a few likely indications for further reflection and contemplation. For present purposes the basic function of clouds is not 'reading' whether they are likely or not to bring or herald rain or shine; for this is not as important as their 'countenance' and gestures in terms of archetypal qualities and attributes, and which we may be able to 'read'.

It is well worth contemplating that the clouds with their variable water-content may be said to depict the outer

A Meditative Approach to Self-knowledge 71

aspect of the Earth's etheric body — and water in all its guises as tides, waves, snow, hail, rain and vapour is invariably associated with etheric forces. The whole atmospheric layer covering the Earth, and to a lesser degree the troposphere, acts as collector, holder and distributor of water, which is necessary for countless kinds of terrestrial life, each of which, by spiritual-scientific definition, possess the appropriate etheric configurations. Moreover, it is no coincidence that the human temperaments are rooted primarily in our etheric or 'life' body, which is largely responsible for all that is rhythmical as well as fluid — two characteristics which are justifiably associated with the power to organize, but sometimes also to relapse into chaos.

Just as our temperaments form a certain mixture appropriate to each individual — one of them is usually dominant, with others as secondary features — so it is with the weather at any given moment in time. The tendency is for meteorologists to express the cloud formations with considerable degrees of exactness, and this almost certainly entails some reference to another type of cloud formation; but as we know all too well, the human psyche is just as unpredictable as the weather! However, upon close examination certain characteristics do emerge which indicate definite major features in terms of both temperaments and weather, and certain judgements can be made with reasonable accuracy and precision. The analogies are certainly present and are worthy of serious contemplation and study.

Just as we have two sets of temperaments, namely, the 'levitational', expansive choleric and sanguine pair as representing the cirrus and cumulus, in the stratus and nimbus we have the 'gravitational', contractive phlegmatic and melancholic types. Thus, in terms of temperament, choleric cirrus is opposite to phlegmatic stratus, just as sanguine cumulus is to melancholic nimbus. The cirrus clouds strive, in a typically choleric, Luciferic manner, to vanish away into and unite with the heavens themselves, whereas the heavily laden Ahrimanic-melancholic nimbus clouds fragment into raindrops and fall to Earth like veritable tears. The often handsome cumulus clouds, although seemingly slow-moving and sedate, bear within themselves air currents as turbulent as any sanguine person's psyche. The phlegmatic stratus clouds, characteristically flat, uninteresting and seemingly dull, also show that they too are capable of change. If nature abhors a vacuum, it must certainly scorn a sky that is always blue.

Chapter 5

Equalizing Positive and Negative

> It is only by rising above ordinary demands of sympathy and antipathy, when we rise to moral ideas and ideals, that we establish our true human nature.[1]

Temperaments positive and negative

When we consider the polar qualities of what is positive and negative with regard to human nature we would be unwise to think immediately of what is merely *neutral*, but rather a process of 'equalizing out'. As we shall see, they represent the contrasting factors of antipathy and sympathy respectively, thus faithfully reflecting and indeed manifesting these opposing soul-forces in our behaviour. At first reading, this sentence seems to express the opposite of what should be the case. Surely, you will say, what is positive has affinities with what is sympathetic, and we commonly associate antipathetic qualities with that which is negative. Notwithstanding this, it must be clearly understood from the outset that the terms *positive* and *negative* are employed here as defined by Rudolf Steiner, and strictly as technical terms within the context of this chapter and elsewhere in the text.[2] (Please refer to this note about this important statement.)

He asserted that sympathy and antipathy are dynamic forces associated with our life of soul, and showed clearly just how they manifest themselves in terms of human behaviour.[3] They are vital factors in our strivings to develop our character throughout our life, and are closely related to our 'ego-ideal' discussed in Chapter 2. Although he did not mention the temperaments as such, it soon becomes clear that, generally speaking, what he described as negative attributes correspond to the Luciferic temperaments (choleric and sanguine), and positive qualities to the Ahrimanic temperaments (phlegmatic and melancholic). Obviously, our temperaments represent the very basis of our actions, for they play an integral part in just how we tackle the problems, difficulties and other concerns of daily life, and how we go about the constant process of decision-making that it entails.

Rudolf Steiner characterized 'positive' people as those who, in their experiences of the outer world, are 'capable of retaining at least to some extent the firmness and security of their inner being, and therefore possess clear-cut ideas and conceptions, certain inclinations one way or another, and feelings from which those impressions cannot move them'. By contrast, 'negative' individuals 'easily submit to the changing impressions of life'; they are inclined to be easily influenced by new ideas and notions they meet in others, and to adopt them even to the extent of making them their own by integrating them into their existing body of knowledge.

We can see at once that we, applying Steiner's criteria, should regard as 'negative' all those people who are open characters, alive to everything that is going on around them, and often responding with enthusiasm and even excitement to that which is novel and attractive—at least to start with. They are often readily converted to new ideas, even to the extent of abandoning their own standpoints which, we may rightly suspect, were acquired only a short time previously. Perhaps they are so captivated by these new notions—considered even after a brief appraisal of them that they are the best thing since sliced bread—that they, with zeal and vigour, immediately try to convert everyone they meet to this wonderful new solution, way, means, process, technique or whatever. They have always known that there just had to be a panacea, *and this is surely it,* and will remain so — until the very next miracle occurs.

It need hardly be said that such people as these represent the flightiest of sanguines, those 'bird-brains' whose feet scarcely touch the ground. They are as it were absorbed by everything that fleetingly attracts them, but they themselves absorb nothing. Small wonder therefore that their minds are in a whirl, for nothing ever seems to 'stick'. Of course this scenario is overblown, but it has to be said that excessively 'negative' people have a willingness to listen. If they are able to train themselves to discern what is worthwhile in what is new or fashionable, they may perhaps learn from it and assimilate it into their very being. This may well resemble a kind of 'revelation', which they immediately recognize and acknowledge as something of permanent value to them and worthy of making their very own.

Of course this means that they have to be, at least for brief periods, positive rather than negative; they probably will, sooner or later, come to acknowledge that in our rapidly changing world, certain principles do indeed hold, and realization of this will be a great comfort to them when it occurs. The time may even come when they find themselves in a position of stubbornly defending firmly established and resolutely defended notions in face of fresh ideas and viewpoints — and thus exhibit blatantly positive attitudes. Whether such notions continue to be attractive will be the acid test.

Patterns of associated characteristics appear

In all this it is easy to see traits and attributes that fit very well into the various sets of characteristics that we recognize as those classified into those of the four temperaments, but it would be unwise to place too much reliance on this concept. With regard to the following table, the attributes represent indications only, but a brief discussion of them is in order.

Factor	Phlegmatic	Choleric	Sanguine	Melancholic
Physique	Eurymorphic	Eurymorphic	Leptomorphic	Leptomorphic
Somatotype	Endomorphic (severe)	Endomorphic (moderate)	Ectomorphic (moderate)	Ectomorphic (severe)
Orientation	Introverted	Extroverted	Extroverted	Introverted
Thinking	Convergent	Divergent	Divergent	Convergent
Social difficulties	Personal	Behavioural	Behavioural	Personal

As regards physique and physiognomy, it is possible to make mistakes of judgement with regard to both eurymorphs and leptomorphs. The researcher W.H. Sheldon insisted that there are only three body types, namely, ectomorphic (lean, slightly muscular), endomorphic (relatively fat, weak muscularity, prominent abdomen) and mesomorphic (powerful musculature, predominantly bony framework). These denotations are dictionary definitions, and are fairly easily recognized as melancholics or sanguines, and phlegmatics and cholerics respectively. The orthodox terminology has been retained, unhelpful and misleading as the characteristics listed are. As discussed by the author in another book,[4] four quite recognizably different temperaments simply will not 'go' into three somatotypes of whatever assortment (solutions to the self-made problem of the orthodox traditionalists are offered in carefully argued form).

Sheldon asserted that he scrutinized 4,000 photographs before reaching his conclusions, thereby proving nothing other than his own inability to distinguish between the typically leptomorphic build of both melancholics and sanguines. From a distance it is of course not always easy to distinguish them, although the somewhat quick and tripping gait of the typical sanguine person is readily perceived by reason of the contrasting slower, more plodding and gangling gait of the average melancholic. Seen close up, the narrow face and somewhat elongated features of the melancholic contrast sharply with the sanguine's often oval or roundish face with regular, aquiline or short and tip-tilted nose. The mobile countenance matches the lively manner of the sanguine.

As for the eurymorphs (phlegmatics and cholerics), the former often have sloping shoulders, whereas those of the latter are usually square, and the relaxed and often plumpish features of the mild-eyed, easy-going phlegmatic person contrast sharply with the taut, tense features and piercing glance of the typical choleric. Moreover, the gait of the latter is quick, firm and purposeful, whereas the average phlegmatic person fairly lollops along.

The matter of inner/outer orientation is more complex than many people imagine. It is easy to discern that Rudolf Steiner, in discussing the positive and negative types of person, their propensities in terms of degree of inner and outer orientation, and so on, is stating what is reasonably obvious in this matter. However, what he says concerning positive and negative characteristics is much more realistic and practical than merely constructing a reasonably obvious principle and leaving it at that.

The lecture referred to earlier[5] was given in 1910, when terms like 'introvert' and 'extrovert' with reference to the human psyche were not yet in common use. According to the *Shorter Oxford Dictionary* such terms were introduced at around 1916, and it is noteworthy that the psychologist Carl

Gustav Jung (1875–1961) made use of them in a book, *Die Psychologie der unbewussten Prozesse*, published in 1917. In November of the same year Rudolf Steiner, in his lecture *Anthroposophy and Psychoanalysis*, poked gentle fun at Jung for as it were 'making official', or at least rendering academically respectable, the readily observable fact that people can easily be roughly categorized into those who are reflective and those who are active—that is to say, into introverts and extroverts respectively.

Since that time these terms have been extended and more refined in their usage. But human nature being as complex as it is, they should be employed as indicative rather than exact terms. At the same time, ideas and concepts are easier to grasp once they have been pointed out, and particularly so when they can be corroborated by reference to other supportive evidence. The whole notion, basic as it is, that we do indeed live in two worlds, the inner and the outer, can be readily seen to support the widespread notion that we represent a duality, namely, body and soul. It would of course be more correct to posit the duality, which is also polar in nature, that of body and spirit, and which by their interaction give rise to a trinity, that of body, soul and spirit. However, the fact remains that we do indeed live in a world of our own creation, one which is amply recognized even by orthodox thinkers.[6]

There are obvious correspondences between the inner/outer orientation of individuals and their ways of thinking. Those whose powers of concentration are good, and whose memories are retentive and reliable, belong to the convergent type of thinker. They find it comparatively easy to handle abstract ideas, and are usually methodical and thorough in their work habits. In general, it may be said that people in this category although not necessarily anti-social in their attitudes and behaviour nevertheless often prefer to occupy themselves with inanimate objects rather than other human beings. It is not surprising that convergent thinkers are good at problem-solving, for it is their habit to think logically. They are inclined to be conventional and orthodox in their attitudes, and to be rather authoritarian, and fixed and rigid in their ways of thinking, feeling and doing.

On the other hand, divergent thinkers often find that their thoughts, so to speak, run away with them, and they often find it difficult to concentrate on the job in hand. This being so, they may find facts and figures difficult to remember, but they are inclined to be artistic, with powers of vivid imagination, and are quick to find solutions to any problems that come their way, very often relying on their intuition rather than reasoning powers. Such people frequently possess keen social consciences, and much prefer to be with their fellow human beings rather than inert and lifeless things.

Divergent people are for the most part active in both mind and body, and their wide range of interests ensure that they accumulate general knowledge at a rapid rate. But frequently they find it difficult to remember much of what they have perhaps only partly learned. They are more flexible in their attitudes than convergents, and are more willing to compromise. There are no appreciable differences in the range of intelligence between these two groups, though it must be said that convergent thinkers, being reflective by nature and with more efficient memories, tend to do better at passing examinations. Generally speaking, introverted people are primarily either phlegmatic or melancholic, and likely to be convergent thinkers, whereas extroverted individuals are usually classifiable as either choleric or sanguine and tend towards divergent habits of thinking.

It stands to reason, generally speaking, that people who

arrange their lives around the promptings and stimuli emanating from the outer world will encounter most of their difficulties from their actions in and reactions to that world. That is to say, it is their actual behaviour in terms of deeds that is likely to give rise to problems. Such people are of course likely to be divergent in their thinking and mental life generally, and extroverted in orientation. Conversely, those whose consuming interests lie in their own inner world will find themselves wrestling mainly with difficulties arising in that domain. They are for the most part introverted in outlook and convergent in their thinking habits. They tend to like their own company and do not mind being alone, whereas their extroverted friends are usually happiest in like-minded company.

Needless to say, human nature being what it is, these proclivities are by no means fixed, and people may well exhibit a mixture of both, swinging between them according to prevailing circumstances, significant life experiences, events, and so on. In terms of positive and negative behaviours regarded in the technical sense in which Rudolf Steiner borrowed and applied them, it is reasonable to contend that those individuals whose nature meets the positive criteria exhibit tendencies that correspond roughly to the two 'closed' melancholic and phlegmatic temperaments. Those whose behaviour satisfies the negative criteria, and are characteristically more 'open' in temperament, correspond to the sanguines and cholerics.

However, it must be reiterated that such matters are far from simple, and it is all too easy to overlook certain aspects which smack of the paradoxical, or the seemingly contradictory. In the case of our two sets of temperaments we encounter further elements of polarity in each one, and these must be addressed.

Getting down to details

It is interesting to surmise just how much the Luciferic cholerics and sanguines, and the Ahrimanic phlegmatics and melancholics, fit into the general overall pattern of *positive* and *negative* put forward by Rudolf Steiner. These pairs of opposites can be adjudged, in the main, to conform to criteria befitting the concepts respectively of *antipathy* (positive) and *sympathy* (negative).

As touched on earlier, at first sight this seems contrary to what people might generally think, but the parameters he cites stand to reason, and are seen to be in every way valid. Positive people are for the most part 'their own' people, who know their own minds, have faith in their convictions and are firm as to their sets of values. They have adopted or developed a definite outlook on life which they feel comfortable with, and live by it. Naturally, they will range from the most dogmatic, stubborn, opinionated and intractable individuals with fixed ideas and rigid views on all topics to those who are open-minded but maintain their reserve, those who have proved—at least to themselves—that their present position with regard to life and the world is satisfactory if provisional, and will maintain it until otherwise convinced. They remain undoubtedly *positive*, steadfast, self-assured, and well-grounded in their principles and their reasons for holding them.

Now in all this they are being thoroughly antipathetic in the sense of instinctively tending to resist whatever situation they are confronted with. Their general attitude is one of circumspection and caution, the whole matter being regarded with varying degrees of objectivity according to their particular way of thinking. The verdict may be fast or slow in coming, but things are not usually taken at their face value, for acknowledgement must be earned or not by reference to reasoning based on further observation and self-debate, and/or the arguments of others. Whether further acquaintance with the matter leads to acceptance or rejection usually rests on their ability to make the supporting evidence agree with their own existing body of knowledge and experience or not, not to mention their prejudices and preconceptions.

At the opposite end of the temperament spectrum we have the two which are the most egotistical — the cholerics and melancholics. The former express this trait by sheer force of outer behaviour. Ambitious and go-ahead, headstrong, energetic and hardworking, they are natural leaders; they like to do things their way, and have things done their way, and no one is allowed to forget it. Extroverted and impulsive, they are eminently suited to accomplishing great deeds in the outer world, but when things go wrong the undeveloped types frequently rave and bluster, whereas the more mature individuals face up to the situation.

Melancholics, on the other hand, whilst equally determined to get their own way, are inclined to resort to under-cover tactics and clever, often devious methods to satisfy their egotistic inclinations. They are skilled schemers and manipulators, and know just when the moment is ripe for plucking at the heartstrings of their victims in order to get their own way. No one is safe from them, except perhaps fellow melancholics who then embark on cat-and-mouse tactics, darkly enjoying every moment of the fray, with each savouring every moment of torment they inflict on the other. Of course, among their ranks we find all sorts of self-sacrificing do-gooders, ranging from inveterate helpers-out and part-time volunteer workers to wealthy philanthropists, and if their egos are pleasurably massaged now and again — and the more often the better, of course—well, only they know the limits of their generosity.

Where the central pair, the sanguines and phlegmatics, are concerned, the first lot have plenty of ideas to spread around, but lack the stickability to carry them out, and the second lot also have plenty of ideas, which they don't talk about, but sell to others if they can, and if they can't they merely sigh and dream of what might have been. Conversely, the ears of the sanguines are always flapping, and their eyes are everywhere, missing nothing. Their interests come and go with bewildering frequency and alacrity, and they are likely to be easily influenced by their friends and others around them, often to the point of modifying their own behaviour to fit what they think will please. In other words, they are for the most part to a greater or lesser degree undeniably *negative*.

Phlegmatics, on the other hand, allow the world to pass them by, not caring very much what people think of them, and quite happy to keep themselves to themselves and stew in their own juice. They know what they like, and like what they know, and can't be very much bothered with what is new or exciting. If some idea dares to attract them, it is closely examined for a long time, turned over and over and perhaps even chewed. If its flavour and substance is passable it may well be swallowed, and more nourishment of similar variety sought out and devoured with equal relish. They thus achieve the rare feat of assimilating something new, which may actually be beneficial to them or even useful and what is more gave them a mild thrill. The whole exercise, they conclude, was thoroughly satisfactory in every respect, and worth repeating. That is to say, they have demonstrated that they are, again to a lesser or greater extent, *positive*.

Positive and negative factors are equally necessary

Ideally, we must be capable of making use, as appropriate and necessary, of all our positive and negative qualities and characteristics if we are to balance out our temperament. The aim—and secret, perhaps—is to get the proportions right. We all possess an instinctive sense of balance and natural justice, and Rudolf Steiner gave some valuable advice in a nutshell of 'if the cap fits, wear it' practicality:

> We should help sanguine people to develop love for and attachment to one personality; we should encourage cholerics to develop respect and esteem for what individuals are able to accomplish; we should show phlegmatics how to work in the interests of other people, and help melancholics to take interest in the destiny of their fellows.[7]

It is the custom and fate of most people merely to 'go with the flow' of whatever proportions they already have, and make little or no conscious effort to change their attitudes and therefore their behaviour. However, as Job observed, man is born to trouble as the sparks fly upward, and life has the habit of providing sufficient trials and tribulations to teach us what we should know. Experience is in many respects the best teacher because it very often teaches us what we may not even want to know.

It must be said, however, that models and paradigms are rarely exact representations of real situations. As hinted earlier, in our pair of positive temperaments we have between them a kind of mini-polarity, and so it is with the negative ones. As Rudolf Steiner pointed out on many occasions, the secondary to the main temperament is its exact opposite. This is why we so often find manic-depressive qualities manifesting in choleric-melancholic types, while excessively sanguine types, mentally and physically exhausted by their frenetic activities, may mercifully relapse into a state of phlegmatic collapse and thereby save the sanity of those around them as well as their own.

We may safely deduce, therefore, that in the case of individuals with positive natures their powers of perception are weak but they are very persevering and resistant to change (melancholics and phlegmatics), whereas in the case of negative characters we find that their powers of perception are strong and those of perseverance weak, so that they are readily disposed to inner change (cholerics and sanguines). We find that all this is in accordance with the assertions of Rudolf Steiner:[8]

Melancholic — perception weak (outer) — retention very strong (inner)
Phlegmatic — perception weakest (outer) — retention weakest (inner)
Sanguine — perception strong (outer) — retention weak (inner)
Choleric — perception strongest (outer) — retention strongest (inner)

As we can see from this table, the complexities of the various temperaments are quite subtle, and tend to be easily overlooked. Melancholics are often, 'slow on the uptake' and can be quite oblivious to what is going on around them. This may be because of their tendency to be occupied with their very strong inner life — and that, it must be said, often concerns exclusively themselves and their own ego-centred world. They turn things over and over in their mind, thus reinforcing and consolidating their already firmly entrenched notions and ideas, views and opinions — hence their innate stubbornness and resistance to anything they do not entirely approve of. They are in danger of 'missing out' by their not being sufficiently 'negative' when they could benefit from being more open.

Phlegmatic people don't particularly care one way or the other about very much, provided their creature comforts are met to their exacting if often idiosyncratic standards. It is often very difficult to discover what makes them 'tick'. What may be exciting or important to their positive associates simply leaves them cold, and although they may listen to other people's ideas with patient deference, the latter would be flattering themselves if they imagined that they had made an impression. For phlegmatics there is an obvious danger here, of course, but if an opportunity for gaining an advantage of some kind is missed, well, 'there are as good fish in the sea as ever came out'.

The sanguines, who have the opposite tendency, never miss a trick and take every chance to assuage their craving for impression, sensation and adventure. It may be said of them, as Mephistopheles did of Faust, that their endeavour is all too often 'to catch but shifting shapes', and are burdened with it almost without realizing it. However, it is as though nature protects them, for impressions come and go so quickly that they remain untouched and unchanged by them. They care intensely about the latest cause for excitement—for a twinkling—but they are so preoccupied with the expectation of further thrills that very little makes a lasting impression.

Those who are mainly choleric find themselves more or less in balance between being positive and negative, according to the influences of their secondary temperament. However, the danger of a 'brainstorm' or an urge towards excess in either direction is always lying in wait, and with it the threat of disaster or the hope of triumph. The notion of 'all or none' is no stranger to such people. What must be the shortest story in the Bible is salutary here:

'There once was a merchant seeking goodly pearls, who, finding one of great price, sold all that he had and bought it.' Cholerics are often a bit too single-minded perhaps, but in disaster their courage, conviction and innate strength regularly render them capable of picking up the pieces and starting all over again.

Mass hysteria and contagious impulses

Naturally, positive and negative propensities are not only confined to individuals but also to whole groups of people *en masse*. A sure sign of this kind of spontaneous behaviour by large numbers of individuals in the form of mass hysteria is a well-known phenomenon, whereby certain events occurring in a group, community or even a whole populace evoke common 'negative' reactions. A striking example of this kind of collective behaviour marked the death and funeral of Diana, Princess of Wales, in the late summer of 1997. Only a tiny percentage of 'mourners' had actually known her personally, yet such was her predominant image that millions who expressed their grief and sorrow felt her death as a personal loss.

More commonly, 'celebrity fever' is likewise evident in the mobbing of pop groups currently in vogue, sports champions, 'stars' of showbiz and other such luminaries by their ardent fans. Quite often things get ugly, especially in the world of football fanatics, rival factions of 'skinheads', and similar. Such frenzied behaviour can be deliberately fostered by the media, especially radio and television sports commentators in their frenetic anticipatory 'build-up' antics, endless play-backs of former glories, and similar thrilling or exciting episodes. Conduct of this kind furnishes ample evidence of how vulnerable and suggestible people can be orchestrated into 'getting high' on sentiment and sensation. The genius of language correctly expresses this contagious lack of firmness and balance that is experienced by people who speak of being 'caught up' or 'carried away' by the 'atmosphere' attending such events, all this being characteristic of actions which regularly demonstrate a certain loss of self-control.

A good example of large numbers of people expressing 'positive' reactions is provided by the so-called 'Dunkirk spirit', when single-minded individuals gather into groups, again as a result of contagious influences, in active response to some kind of emergency, disaster or other crisis. At that time in 1940 the whole British people braced themselves against the consequences, imagined or real, of the evacuation of their defeated army from northern France. The sense of unity in face of calamity, the strong feeling of camaraderie which pervaded the entire country, and the mood of genuine fellowship, of willingly shared hardships and dangers brought about by enemy action, revealed a breaking down of constraints which resembled in certain respects the typical reactions to the death of Diana, Princess of Wales.

The now little-used term *esprit de corps* does not fully describe the feelings of intense loyalty which I experienced during my wartime years as a private soldier, when my cap-badge served for me, as it did for other members of my 'unit', as both focus and inspiration. Conduct 'beyond the call of duty' was expected as a matter of course. Everyone 'mucked in', and the one-for-all and all-for-one ethic was taken for granted. Some 'glory boys' were perhaps overly keen to demonstrate their mateyness, their die-hard attitude of backs-to-the-wall solidarity and stubbornness of resistance in face of the enemy, but their intentions were sincere. So there was a certain degree of 'wallowing' in the sharing of emotive reactions both negative and positive, in respect of the two sets of circumstances exemplified; for with tears dried and the war won, memories fade and the former inhibitions reassert themselves.

On a smaller scale and to a lesser degree, although no less important for that, are to be seen the various clubs, societies, associations and suchlike which foster particular interests in a 'negative' way, operating as it were in a centrifugal, expansionist fashion. They introduce or exchange ideas in a thoroughly open-minded manner, eager and willing to learn whatever they can from one another by sharing experiences and extending their concerns for mutual benefit inasmuch as they represent a kind of extended family, which is all wholesome, well and good.

The opposite attitude to this is of course one that is equally thoroughly 'positive', and characterized by the kind of 'mob mentality' exhibited by passionately loyal bands of football supporters of a particular team who are prepared to give battle in defence of their favourites. They represent a tightly integrated, closed group whose horizons are limited by a strongly centripetal 'nuclear' force of self-interest and ambition to be top dog.

Public demonstrations by opposing factions which lead to disturbances or even riots also illustrate the operation of 'positive' characteristics. This 'be my brother or I'll batter you to death' attitude is emotive rather than rational, and has more to do with the 'survival of the fittest' ethos than one furthering the public good. This is hardly a desirable programme.

Rudolf Steiner must have the last word:

> We cannot rise to a higher level unless we leave a lower positive level, and change to a negative attitude, in which he absorbs some new content. This he carries through with himself, so that he becomes positive on a higher level. If we

observe nature rightly, we can see how world wisdom obliges us to pass from positive to negative and from negative to positive.⁹

Chapter 6

Smoothing the Mixture

When from thought, which is universal, and feeling, which can be common to all, we turn to our will which always brings us back to the ego, we find a definite place assigned to us, and from this centre we must direct our lives.[1]

Putting ourselves into proper perspective

It is to their great detriment that most people in the so-called civilized world do not realize that we human beings are primarily spiritual in nature, and only secondarily creatures of flesh and blood. It follows therefore that our real home is the spiritual world rather than the earthly world, and that at the present time we are sojourning visitors rather than permanent dwellers on our planet. It is vital that this fact be fully understood. Our ego is our only truly spiritual member, and it is important to realize that what we usually refer to in everyday affairs as our ego is in reality a pale representation of our real Ego, our immortal, indestructible 'Higher Self' which never departs from its actual home in the spiritual world.[2] Rudolf Steiner gave this inspiring verse on the occasion of the founding of the Anthroposophical Society in Great Britain in London on 2 September 1923:

I gaze into the Darkness.
In it there arises Light—
Living Light.
What is this Light in the Darkness?
It is I myself in my reality.
This reality of the 'I'

Does not enter into my Earthly life.
I am but a picture of it.
But I shall find it again
When with good will for the Spirit
I shall have passed through the Gate of Death.[3]

Our true Ego is enormously powerful, but most of this power is held as it were in reserve, for at our present overall state of development it cannot be fully deployed. Our true Ego remains, indestructible as it is, essentially inviolable, as the enduring agent which brings about changes in order to serve its purposes in each individual human being by working through the members which are subservient to it, namely, the astral body, etheric body and physical body. Itself utterly moral, its task is to garner all our earthly experiences, more particularly that of death, which are passed on in turn to the members of the higher hierarchies, none of whom has experienced death, and indeed neither can nor will.

Rudolf Steiner's sevenfold configuration of the human being in his book *Theosophy* may be regarded as the definitive model, and this can be extended to indicate the developmental stages of the Earth as well, as described in his book which also sets out certain other basic tenets of anthroposophy, namely, *Occult Science – An Outline*:

1. Physical-material body — Old Saturn
2. Etheric or Life body — Old Sun
3. Astral body — Old Moon
4. Ego or 'I', as soul kernel — Earth
5. Spirit-self as transmuted astral body — Jupiter
6. Life-spirit as transmuted etheric body — Venus
7. Spirit man as transmuted physical body — Vulcan

Now one of the principal long-term tasks of the ego is the ennobling or spiritualizing of our 'lower' vehicles that we have already acquired, and this is an ongoing long-term evolutionary process. As the table above indicates, the principle closest to the spirit-filled ego is the astral body, which is also the 'youngest' and most akin to it in terms of its essential nature. This means that it is 'easier' to work on, resulting on the soul level in the engendering of the sentient soul, the intellectual, rational or mind soul, and the consciousness or spiritual soul, which bear the particular influences characteristic of the intrinsic nature of the astral body itself as well as those of the etheric and physical bodies respectively. The connections of these soul-members, each with its particular nature and function, are readily seen to be applicable to our soul-forces of feeling, thinking, and willing respectively.

However, the work does not stop there, for with further refining of these soul members the three spiritual members are created, or prepared for in seminal fashion, namely, spirit-self from our astral nature, life-spirit from our etheric principles, and spirit-man from our physical constitution. Now it is these three spiritual members which, according to the grand scheme of things outlined by Rudolf Steiner, will be ripe for regular development in maturational terms during the coming three evolutionary stages of the Earth itself, and by implication the whole of humanity as well. These are usually referred to as the Jupiter, Venus and Vulcan stages, which will then complete the schedule of the seven stages listed in the table.[4]

It is at the present stage of the evolution of the Earth that its constitution—and again by strict implication that of the human physical body—is at its most dense. Accordingly, we have been obliged to develop bodily senses capable of apprehending an environment consisting in its outer manifestation of matter. We are not normally able to access the spiritual worlds because this is rendered impossible by what Rudolf Steiner often referred to as 'the veil of the senses'. However, the present situation, whereby the spiritual world which exists behind all that is physical/mineral in composition has become closed to us, will be reversed during the impending stages of Earthly and human development.

These will reveal themselves as they unfold as the result of our acquisition by ordinary evolutionary processes of that facility which is at present regarded as more advanced, namely, the powers of supersensible perception of 'higher' worlds acquired by means of esoteric training. In other words, the eventual unfolding by humanity of what is now known as Imagination, Inspiration and Intuition will take place during the evolutionary periods referred to earlier as Jupiter, Venus and Vulcan respectively by the agency of standard evolutionary processes.

It should be clear from all this just how important it is to know how we each stand with regard to our relatively minor task of balancing out our temperaments. Achieving this could mark the very first step on a very long journey, and puts our strivings to bring it about in sharp perspective. Moreover, further 'balancing out' operations and procedures await us in kamaloka and the soul and spiritual worlds after death as a matter of course.[5] As a glance at the table above will serve to show, the comparatively easy balancing act involving our temperaments is part of the whole evolutionary process which includes the Earth as well as ourselves.

The important universal *law of self-correction* is evident in every balancing operation, the main principles of which can be clearly discerned in the workings of karma or self-created destiny.[6] But it has many other applications in daily life as well as cosmic events, as reflection will show. Obviously, we are capable of changing only ourselves. We may influence, and be influenced, by others, but in the last resort we are each responsible for our own stage of development.

Inner promptings and incentives

Not only is our 'ordinary' ego our most spiritual member, it is also the youngest; that is to say, in terms of the evolutionary process it is our latest acquisition, and as such our least developed. It would be no exaggeration to assert that, compared with our older members—astral, etheric and physical—it is positively embryonic. Our wonderfully organized and amazingly efficient physical constitution, rendered competent by an equally remarkable etheric body upon which it is entirely dependent and by which it is fully maintained, is so precision-built as to be able to run itself. Indeed, it is so amazingly analogous to a machine that it is actually regarded as such by modern science. In normal circumstances we simply take our corporeal nature (our combined physical and etheric organization) for granted; for it is only when its regular functions are impeded by accident, illness or other disorder that we become most aware of it.

It is from our true Ego or Higher Self that we receive our more lofty ideals, moral impulses, altruistic tendencies, and all that we designate as 'good' in the sense of social as well as individual welfare. It is our 'ordinary' ego, which is closer to the field of operations in the earthly world, by which we assess our progress, or lack of it, by pondering past triumphs and disasters as objectively and discriminatingly as we can. If little or no advancement is made, the urge to arrange matters so that this may become possible appears as it were unbidden, without prompting from others. The incentive to raise our moral standards is strengthened, and with it a fresh determination and resolve to attain higher standards of altruism, and fellow-feeling; and the stronger our ego the more likely we are to succeed in our efforts. These inner promptings may with some justification be attributable to our true Ego.

If this becomes the case it is to our advantage, for then the cosmic law of self-correction begins to work. Rudolf Steiner asserted that whenever egotism in individuals takes a wrong turn the time comes when they become aware of its powers of self-annihilation, and eventually realize that altruism brings its own rewards.[7] As the ego grows stronger and more conscious of this fact, so will its powers of self-denial and self-subordination in favour of others, as and when wise and appropriate. Reflection along these lines will bring the realization that the more we give ourselves up to self-love the more barren we become in our inner life. We all experience the struggle between our higher nature represented by our true Ego, which is capable of self-sacrifice, modesty and humility, and our lower nature, with its selfish desires and its urge to manipulate the environment to our own advantage, of which we may or may not be fully conscious.

Make sure you really are in charge

If the ego is to maintain a balance between the opposing influences of Lucifer and Ahriman it must be strong. We should be able — indeed must be able — to stand firm within our own being, to actually feel that we are integrated within ourselves and in command of our faculties, particularly in our power to think clearly and logically, and in our will. The ego, as the primary agent, must also be the source of motivation for action, and expresses itself through the will, which means that we must possess sufficient determination to tackle the task before us to the very best of our strength and ability—and complete it.

Whilst in the supersensory worlds after death we are in constant activity, and the common gravestone inscription RIP (*Resquiescat In Pace*—May he/she Rest In Peace) has a very hollow ring. Not surprisingly, our strivings whilst on Earth are also seemingly endless, and there is little comfort in the ordinary sense to be got from Rudolf Steiner's verse:

> To us it is given
> At no stage ever to rest.
> They live and they strive, the active
> Human beings from life unto life,
> As plants grow from springtime
> To springtime—ever aloft,
> Through error upward to truth,
> Through fetters upward to freedom,
> Through illness and death
> Upward to beauty, to health and to life.[8]

It is debatable whether modern life provides much opportunity for people's ego strength to develop as it needs to—and just when genuine strength of character is demanded by it. Even the ordinary vicissitudes of life prove too much for many people, young and adult alike, as indicated by the increasing numbers of individuals seeking medical help because of panic attacks, depression, the need to escape from their predicament, and so on. The rapid changes in the political, social and economic life of the country leave people bewildered and anxious. They are continually told what to do, what to think, and even what to feel, by the appropriate 'experts' and commentators, politicians, radio and television presenters, programme makers and entertainers alike.

Children are being increasingly robbed of their childhood, growing up to become adults who are weak-willed, and wavering in opinion and lacking in true powers of judgement. This comes about as a direct result of the growing tendency to encourage children to 'express themselves' prematurely, when all they are capable of expressing has been planted in their minds by their parents and teachers. The myriad influences assailing them from all sides, particularly from the mass media, are more insidious than ever before, and whilst older people look on in dismay, they know that there is little they can do about it.

However, as a result of ordinary life experiences and learning from them, we all become more mature in our judgements and, as we grow ever older, more compassionate towards others and more charitable in the widest sense. Life has the effect of 'knocking our corners off', and we realize that it is indeed only when we rise above the ordinary demands of sympathy and antipathy, when we actively strive to implement moral ideas and ideals in the world and society, that we establish our truly human nature, as Steiner averred.

It would be absurd if we remained constantly negative or stubbornly positive, for we should learn to discriminate and deliberately and actively choose when we should adopt a positive or a negative attitude towards a given situation, and most people instinctively know this. The cultivation of sensitivity in this respect of itself helps us to even out our sympathies and antipathies, and hence to smooth over our more resistant personality excesses by not indulging ourselves in them.

The heart as an organ of balance

Psychologists, educationists and others would do well to study the implications of Rudolf Steiner's observation that

Smoothing the Mixture 99

feeling is thinking in reserve, and also willing in reserve.[9] Equidistant between the two behavioural poles of willing (Luciferic) and thinking (Ahrimanic) lies feeling, which is truly representative of our soul-life. From its central position between thinking and willing, feeling is of course nicely placed to be influenced by, and in turn to influence, both of these opposite soul-qualities, and hence our faculties of sympathy and antipathy, which are in ceaseless oscillation during our waking hours. The human heart (feeling) acts as balancing agent between our head (thinking) and our metabolic-limbs system (willing). This is a typical indication of how the whole world is a result of the working of countless manifestations of the working of balance.

Nature is for the most part investigated by scientific methodologies and interpreted by materialistic philosophies, and these are obviously associated with the typically Ahrimanic qualities of forming and structuring — in this case logically conceived and systematically presented concepts proper to our soul-faculty of *thinking*. With equal validity the whole of nature could be regarded as the result of the workings of the cosmic *will*, manifesting as a colossal work of art that provides the sphere for reciprocating acts of will in the form of action or reaction. This involves the Luciferic attributes of inciting the desire for deed, energetically deployed for the most part in the selfish interests of the doer.

The principle of *feeling* arises between these two poles of soul-activity, thus giving rise to opportunities for the exercising of sympathetic subjectivity (Lucifer) as well as antipathetic objectivity (Ahriman). It is the balancing principle innate in our soul faculty of feeling that endeavours constantly to stabilize and bring into harmony our faculties of thinking and willing, so that we become increasingly capable of accomplishing wisdom-filled deeds.

Ahriman's abode in us is concentrated in the brain and in the central nervous system, which supports it as our organ of thinking. Lucifer's domain is for the most part our vascular system and metabolic-limbs system, in which our life of will is centred. Neither faction is present in a directive capacity in our rhythmic system which lies between the other two systems and is, by long tradition and in fact, the seat of our life of feeling. The heart, with which is connected the life-sustaining blood, has obviously important associations with the metabolic system, and hence with the sympathetic, subjective will-nature, and the lungs bear antipathetic, objective relationships with the outside world by reason of the air we breathe.

The heart is known to be a kind of inner 'sense-organ' for the whole human organism; and part of its function is, organically and in soul-spiritual terms, to strive to maintain a state of balance between the head system and the metabolic system, between thinking and willing, and—at least as far as this is possible—between sympathy and antipathy. The heart, in its centrally placed zone of power, is therefore ideally placed for counter-influencing them in turn within its ability, perhaps enhancing them or curtailing them. The modifying influence of the heart as a balancing agent tends to resist excessively Luciferic temptations. At worst, these take the form of giving expression to the kind of actions that manifest an unreasonably high proportion of egotistical *will*-activity, such as excessively headstrong and domineering behaviour, perhaps incorporating unrealistic schemes, extravagant ambitions and exaggerated selfish actions of all kinds.

Where Ahriman is concerned, it is the *thinking*-activity that becomes subject to various aberrations. This may well manifest itself in speculative thinking, excessive emphasis on purely intellectual issues and such stock-in-trade as abstractions, dubious hypotheses, pedantry, over-dependence on purely empirical research, thinking along logical-positive or deterministic lines, and suchlike. It is virtually impossible for Ahriman, bereft of any kind of feeling, even to comprehend what stirs in the human heart. Lucifer knows very well that every kind of passion and emotion reside there: love, hate, fear, courage, hope, despair, joy, sorrow, optimism, pessimism, depression, elation, and so on. Any of these, and countless other soul-sensations when experienced to excess, spells trouble.

The inference is clear that we should make every effort to discover just how we ourselves relate to Lucifer and Ahriman, and to take their influences into consideration by means of greater and more discerning self-knowledge. The problem here is that of subjectivity. Try as hard as we may, it is virtually impossible to remain entirely objective about ourselves, and this is why a thorough knowledge of the temperaments, as providing various points of reference, is strongly to be recommended.

Monitoring our own behaviour

Every attempt should be made to be as objective as possible about our own main, secondary and subsidiary temperaments by means of reflection and self-criticism, and efficient means of achieving this is by employing the 'backward review' technique just before going to sleep at night. The main thing to remember is that the most significant events of the day should pass before the inner observant eye *in reverse order*, and in as much detail as possible, whilst disregarding trivial or minor happenings. We should try to observe ourselves as if by a third party and from above, and to ensure that no event of real significance is overlooked. Such an exercise should not take up more than ten minutes or so, and although this may sound relatively effortless, in practice it is all too easy for our mind to wander from the strict pattern of events as they occurred, or we may even fall asleep. If we persist, however, our powers of concentration and our ability to form mental images will improve considerably, and by thus observing our actions more closely by means of such a review we may well become better people.

As remarked earlier, it is uncommonly difficult to be entirely objective about anything. But the cold reserve of the cerebral melancholics and the bland indifference and caution of the phlegmatics generally ensure that nothing rash or impulsive, not to mention imprudent, is seriously contemplated. Such folk are not, of course, paragons of objective virtue, for the counterbalance swings in with a vengeance. They may be objective about the outer world, but they are thoroughly subjective about themselves and their own little world. They may not have illusions about their environment, but delusion may well reign within.

As we have already seen, the more passive, reflective, 'inner' individuals, the typical convergent thinkers, are those of melancholic or phlegmatic propensities. Melancholics are so innately self-involved that they are generally happy with their own company, and may resent interference and distraction. Phlegmatics don't like to be bothered about anything that does not coincide with their idiosyncratic interests, and by the same token will not be inclined to bother other people unnecessarily. In their own way, phlegmatics and melancholics are 'closed in': melancholics preoccupied with their own physical body with all its dullness and heaviness, and phlegmatics content to be left to stew in their own juices.

Obversely, it is to be expected that the more active, extroverted, energetic individuals, those who tend to think divergently—and they include so-called lateral thinkers—are sociable in nature, and tend towards 'flowing over' into their environment in acts of will, mostly leaving their mark temporarily (sanguines) and rather more permanently (cholerics). In any case their qualities of creativity, including artistic creativity, enthusiasm, zeal and vision (with just a hint of the visionary, perhaps), are unquestionably Luciferic in character. Such characters find it difficult to be objective with regard to the outer world, because they are, so to speak, too 'close' to it, too involved, too much wrapped up in it. They may survey whatever tasks need to be addressed, and plan accordingly in great and sufficient detail. But any such objectivity is all too often swept away by some grandiose, pretentious or high-flown scheme or other that amounts to little more than castles in the air. So when the crash comes, in terms of shattered pride and self-esteem, or perhaps in monetary terms, objectivity-plus cuts in, and a few well-deserved lessons are learned.

Beware Lucifer and Ahriman

Rudolf Steiner pointed out that Lucifer and Ahriman work together, or at least appear to. In any case you may be sure that if you get a whiff of Luciferic enticement, Ahriman will be around to scent it too, and get you by the scruff of your neck. Lucifer, as light-bearer, is responsible for our capacity for sense-perception and hence our waking consciousness by reason of our astral body. He it is who 'fires us up' with fervour and enthusiasm, who aids us in our creative thinking, and everything associated with enlightenment or illumination. In a very real sense, he is the god of tomorrow, who imparts the qualities of hope, eagerness, anticipation and ardour. In addition, Lucifer rules in our passions; we have him to thank for our intensities of love and hate, our raptures, blisses, ecstasies and thrills, and all that we experience as euphoric. Needless to say, therefore, he is above all the god of temptation and enticement.

The dichotomous model of ourselves as being of Ahrimanic propensities (corporeal nature comprising physical and etheric bodies) and Luciferic influences (soul-spiritual nature comprising astral body and ego) is a basic one, and needs to be kept in mind. We are very much awake in our thinking, but we are dreaming in our feeling life and unconscious in the activation of our will impulses. The danger in all this is of course the tendency for the astral forces, impulses and stimuli to gain precedence over the ego itself, when the reverse situation should obtain. The etheric body, sandwiched as it were between the physical body below and the astral body above, is well placed for influencing both. It is evident from observation and experience, however, that although co-operation with and power over the patient, long-suffering physical body is abundantly plain, influence of any significance over the astral body is not very apparent. Nevertheless, our etheric body is constantly seeking preponderance over our astral nature.[10]

It is at this interfacing plane in the human constitution that Lucifer and Ahriman actually confront each other. The astral forces, which are centrifugal in their mode of operation, strive to work their way more deeply into the etheric body, and the etheric forces with their centripetal dynamics attempt to gain ascendancy over the astral nature. In this circumstance the etheric body suffers ascendancy by the older physical body in the lower nature, and in our higher nature the astral body is subject to the preponderance of the ego, both thereby bringing pressure to bear towards the central area of confrontation between Lucifer and Ahriman. We are, at all times and in all circumstances striving to maintain a state of equilibrium between Ahriman, ensconced in our lower, corporeal nature, and Lucifer, equally snugly entrenched in our higher, soul-spiritual nature. Ahriman is by intention atomistic and fragmentary, and it must not be forgotten that he invented the 'divide and conquer' strategy, and frequently succeeds in obtaining his aims and ends by this means.

It would be futile to attempt to set out in detail just how to modify our temperaments in anything but general terms; going into particulars is the task of each individual. However, a smattering of hints concerning ways and means of how to go about balancing them out has been given throughout the text with the helpful intention of assisting in the ongoing task of getting wise to ourselves as well as other people. We are all in the process of metamorphosing ourselves, with the ego as agent, for either better or worse, and when the point of balance is reached with regard to a certain matter, the time is ripe for attaining to a further stage, whatever that may be. The particular objective having been reached, we shall probably be able to utilize the situation as a basis for a further task.

In all this it is as well that we know what we are doing when any balancing out of our temperaments is seriously embarked upon, for we are lifting ourselves out of the realms of instinctual operation into that of conscious behaviour, thus incurring the demand that we create our own points of reference. Rudolf Steiner gave this warning:

> We are still far from the time when the wisdom instinctively implanted in humanity as a divine impulse will be raised into consciousness. Hence in our age people are liable to err ... and it is now particularly necessary that the great dangers to be found at this point should be counteracted by a spiritual conception of the world, so that what humanity once possessed as instinctive wisdom may now become conscious wisdom.[11]

We should not of course rely on our temperaments alone, for we must resist any tendency to become enslaved by them. Rather should we do all we can to strengthen our ego in order to *command* whichever is appropriate in a given situation, and bring them into harmony by exercising our will in a wise manner. As we know, our will pole is the Luciferic, comprising as it does our choleric and sanguine proclivities. Ideally, we should be ever sensitive and alert to the appropriateness of any action we carry out, so that what we do should ultimately be in the service of the divine powers. Lucifer would have us be good and moral, but act out of a kind of spurious freedom of the kind associated with compulsive knee-jerk reaction prompted by sentiment rather than genuine, self-effacing love.

Our Ahrimanic pole, consisting of our phlegmatic and melancholic propensities, serves our powers of thinking, the means by which we obtain knowledge. This necessarily forms the basis of wisdom, which is none other than knowledge permeated by genuine altruistic love. Our aim should always be to 'think with the heart', thus combining will and wisdom in all our dealings by harnessing the powers of Lucifer and Ahriman in a thoroughly Christian way and making them work for us in our strivings to achieve equilibrium.

A few sly reminders for the wobbly

As already mentioned, our temperaments are entrenched in our etheric body, and as an important characteristic of etheric forces is their association with the factor of time, rapid results are not to be expected. As we know, the phlegmatic temperament is itself rooted in our etheric body, and its qualities and attributes are those which are advantageous in comparison to those of the other three temperaments.[12] In fact, as Rudolf Steiner stated, those who have a phlegmatic temperament already possess a certain degree of equanimity and stability as well as a degree of self-knowledge, and this is decidedly to their advantage.

A commonly held view is that possessors of a sound phlegmatic disposition are to be pitied rather than envied. They personify the blandness of the taste of water itself. But it is fortunate for us all that we are able to energize our phlegmatic propensities in that regard, and not tire of its flavourlessness. Apparently unresponsive to many a stimulus that would excite people endowed with rather more lively qualities, the dull and apathetic phlegmatics are in fact highly sensitive to atmosphere and environment as well as the 'presence' of others. The dislike of their own equilibrium being disturbed is usually extended to others, for to them harmony both inner and outer is paramount. Their main handicap is their sheer inability, or at least reluctance, to instigate change in either themselves or their surroundings, but when pressures become too great in one area or another they are just as likely to explode as sink into ruinous phlegmatic collapse.

The companion temperament to the phlegmatic, even if for the sole reason of being the other with innate 'Ahrimanic' propensities, is the melancholic. A prominent characteristic of people with this disposition is their readiness to criticize and call to account. That includes themselves if they are so disposed, but also other people, and are capable of turning their qualities of rigidity, contrariness, and self-inflicted misery to the benefit of others. Melancholics are inclined habitually to call up memories of past experiences and to ponder on their significance in their lives, and thus they are well placed for self-examination and genuine self-knowledge. Depth of character is a definite asset to them unless, of course, they dive so deeply into themselves that they find it difficult to surface. When they do, they should endeavour to make for the shallow end of themselves, and try to have a little fun—just a bit to start with, naturally.

Diametrically opposed to melancholics in terms of temperament are the sanguines, and if they are able to cross the divide occasionally when opportunities present themselves, and indulge in a little flippancy and superficiality now and again, or sometimes even challenge their strongest convictions—well, they will at least have garnered a few more memories to muse over.

Choleric people believe that changing themselves in any way is not only unnecessary, but definitely disadvantageous. They are self-confident and self-assured, and have plenty of drive and ambition; the will to succeed at almost any cost is built into them. It is not for them to change—the world must be changed to suit them and, what is more, they have the temperamental wherewithal to change it. Lucifer is a consummate inspirer of the will, and with it sufficient hot-bloodedness for it to become action.

Ahriman, as master manipulator of the laws of thought, seeks to persuade us that our inner world is the only real world. Seldom stopping to think, or looking before they leap, cholerics are not very prone to learning from past experiences, however unexpected or unlooked for; it is simply not their style. As inveterate know-alls, they never listen, but are ever ready and willing to tell you where you went wrong. After all, as Mr, Mrs, Miss or Ms Wonderful, perfection comes as standard—naturally.

Those happy-go-lucky folk with sanguine temperaments are not worried one bit that their nerves are out on stalks, because generally they do not even realize that this is the case. Their inability to concentrate on anything for long is helped (or hindered) by Lucifer, for theirs is the airy realm.

The image of butterflies is a superb one where sanguines are concerned. Their flight may seem erratic, irregular and unpredictable, but they very often settle on the finest of flowers.

They may find it very difficult to balance themselves in the orthodox fashion, but never underestimate them. They will dazzle you with their sheer brilliance, turn on the charm, run rings around you and, before you know it, you've lost your innocence and much else besides. Of course, the obverse may well obtain on occasions, and the sight of a crestfallen sanguine, when they have been out-manoeuvred and driven into a corner, is not a happy one. Perhaps they should try sitting before a beehive — for a little longer than merely a second or two — and contemplate just why it is that its occupants seem so contented and happy with their lot that they don't even bother to come out and sting them.

Chapter 7

The Greeks Had a Word for It

> As a study precisely of the temperaments will show, the most beautiful relations can arise between human beings when one person beholds another and is not only able to fathom the riddle they present, but also understands how to let love flow from individuality to individuality.[1]

Changing for the better

Whether we like it or not, or even realize it or not, our temperamental configuration is integral to our being and is closely bound up with our whole self-created destiny. To make a trivial but nonetheless telling comparison, we possess in varying proportions the characteristics of our four temperaments as being 'dealt' to us — as we deserve — after the manner of the varying values of playing cards within their four suits. Earlier I drew attention somewhat waggishly to the two red (diabolic — Luciferic) suits of Hearts and Diamonds, and two black (satanic — Ahrimanic) suits of Clubs and Spades. Life is, with some justification perhaps, regarded by many people as a game, and how they 'play' their 'hands' in terms of temperament is entirely up to each individual according to his or her knowledge and ability. The analogy is far from being exact, of course, for what is 'won' in terms of cards means that other players have 'lost', but there always will be winners and losers nevertheless.

It is of course possible to change our disposition, or rather consciously choose whichever attribute of the temperament(s) with which we have been endowed that is desirable and appropriate for our personal behaviour at any particular time. Actions always speak louder than words, as we know, and try as we might we cannot hide our true nature for long. We are forced to acknowledge the truth of the words 'by their fruits shall ye know them'. This may be a slow process, but we possess a great advantage if we get to know ourselves, our strengths and weaknesses, our foibles and imperfections—those we admit and those we don't.

However, there is nothing better than a little training in this direction, and Rudolf Steiner was tireless in giving many valuable indications for seeking knowledge of ourselves by turning outwards as much as inwards, several of which have already been introduced or discussed. Here is another:

> In the boundless Without
> Find thyself, O Man!
> In the innermost Within
> Feel the boundless Worlds!
>
> So will it be revealed:
> Nowhere the Riddle of Worlds is solved,
> Save in the being of Man.[2]

And for good measure, because of the mistaken if popular notion that it is only by following an exclusively 'inner path' in the search for our 'real selves' that we are able to succeed, here is yet one more:

> Perceive the secrets of thy soul
> In the countenance
> The wide world turns towards thee.
> Perceive the living essence of the World
> In the countenance
> Imprinted by it on thy soul.[3]

We should not have to remind ourselves constantly that we are primarily spiritual beings and only secondarily creatures of the earth. It is necessary always to be on guard against allowing the sheer materialism of modern culture to cloud our vision. Rudolf Steiner listed seven preconditions for making progress in the understanding of ourselves and the world, but also for establishing sound personal relationships, which in turn furthers the health of society itself.[4] There are no incompatibilities between Christian and other moral doctrines, rightly understood, and the requirements for character development and esoteric training in spiritual science itself. What is of the greatest possible importance is that both paths lead eventually to an understanding and appreciation of the mission of the Christ Being for the Earth and humanity as one of cosmic-historical proportions rather than narrowly sectarian-religious.[5]

All this being so, it is reasonable to contend that individuals, whether progressing along the path of spiritual development by way of knowledge or that of observing the highest principles of the Christian—or other—faith, are all aiming to achieve the situation where they can truly say, *yet I live, no longer I, but Christ lives in me*, in the meaning of Paul (Galatians 2:20). We have seen all along that Christ, as the Representative of Man, the 'firstborn among many brethren' (Romans 8:29) in the sense of both Paul and Rudolf Steiner as well as numerous mystics and divines, has as part of His task the keeping of Lucifer and Ahriman in balance on a cosmic scale. In order for us to be able to do likewise, it is essential that we recognize these opposing powers by their characteristics, and these we have discussed.

Now we have argued all along that the choleric and sanguine temperaments exhibit to a considerable extent the attributes of Lucifer, whereas the phlegmatic and melancholic temperaments relate to those of Ahriman. From this it follows that we, in so far as we bear Christ within us in the Pauline sense and through our understanding of the temperaments, should strive to discern the Christ in people we meet and interact with. By reason of this, we should further endeavour to adjust our own behaviour with the end in view of enabling such individuals, as and when opportunities present themselves, better to understand themselves and their fellows. In this respect it may be asserted that knowledge acquired in understanding our own temperament serves as a guide for our understanding other people's also.

The abstract methodologies of the modern psychology laboratory are bound to suffer shortcomings because the experimenters do not acknowledge the true nature of ourselves as spiritual beings, as their rejection of the ancient tried and tested doctrine of the four temperaments demonstrates. Many people who have no knowledge of spiritual science may have an instinctive urge towards what they can only call 'character development', and of course this is always for the benefit of others rather than ourselves. They may also realize that very often their own disposition gets in the way, but do not know what to do about 'improving' it.

The traditional sources of instruction and support for moral advancement appear in the guise of religious doctrines, which do of course serve as a valuable foundation for self-development and spiritual enlightenment. It is profoundly regrettable that today's materialistic scientists are 'missing out' on what spiritual science has to offer. They are clever rather than wise, and true wisdom always bears within it the content of morality. Concerning all this Rudolf Steiner had this to say:

By acquiring knowledge of human nature we learn to understand both the faults and the virtues of our fellow human beings. Such wisdom, born of living insight into the world, passes into the blood, into action and will. And human love, so called, is born of such wisdom.[6]

Loving our neighbour

Self-knowledge and understanding of how we express ourselves through our individual attributes, qualities and general disposition is bound to result in the knowledge and understanding of our fellows and their conduct, and this in turn affects our own social behaviour. The most important feature of life itself is human relationships between individuals, in that the principle of love permeates the whole of society in countless ways. Everything hinges on our developing a pure and unconditional love for our fellows, trying to meet their needs whatever they may be, whether asked for or not. This means taking a genuine interest in them, so that we are able to bring unaffected goodness into practical aspects of daily life as love in action.

As the soul is the arena for the interplay between sympathy and antipathy, our likes and dislikes in all their variety figure large in our everyday life. Reflection will show that whatever is present in our *antipathy* tends in the general direction of our faculty of *thinking*, whereas our *sympathy* inclines towards our faculty of *willing*. These faculties come directly under the influence of our ego, and it is our sacred duty to strive ceaselessly and faithfully to carry out acts of good will and genuine charity. In today's pain-wracked world this message of compassion is answered by the many altruistic workers who are to be found wherever there is disaster and calamity, whether natural or man-made. Rudolf Steiner expressed such feelings of genuine empathy with our fellows in stark terms:

So long as thou dost feel the pain
Which I am spared,
The Christ, unrecognized,
Is working in the World.
For weak still is the Spirit
Whilst each is capable of suffering
Only through his own body.[7]

The key to all this is to be found in the quotation for this chapter, where Rudolf Steiner mentions our ability to acquire understanding of how to let *love* flow from one individual to another. It need scarcely be said that this is the kind of freely given, unselfish, unconditional or Christian love in the sense of the Greek word *agape,* which is used by the apostle Paul in the well-known eulogy on love in his first letter to the Corinthians, Chapter 13. Sloppy, maudlin sentimentality is not in any way expressive of genuine love; rather should we strive to recognize other individuals for what they are, and love them regardless in the sense of *agape,* for this is a demand of the coming Age.[8] Love in this sense is not so much an ordinary emotion as what may be termed 'heart-wisdom' born of true understanding of the needs—rather than mere wants—of both ourselves and others. Rudolf Steiner also had much to say about love, describing it as being 'the child of the spirit' and as 'the moral sun of the world'. There is no doubt about the enormous power of love, in the name of which in its everyday sense much unhappiness as well as happiness is brought about.

Rudolf Steiner's closing remarks in his lecture *The Four Temperaments,* which he gave in various venues during the winter of 1908/09, repay close study and contemplative work. He spoke earnestly about making every effort to *understand* our fellows as individuals and not merely pass them by. Opportunities for establishing truly harmonious relationships should not be missed, and his words constitute a real challenge to every student of spiritual science:

> In spiritual science it is so that when one soul confronts another, asking for love, love is given; if a soul asks for something else, that too is given. Thus do we create the basis of a true social life through a true wisdom of life... Love is the blossom and fruit of a life quickened by spiritual science. That is why spiritual science may justly claim that it creates the soil for *human love*—the fairest goal of the human race. Our sympathy, our love, the way we meet and behave towards each individual person—all this will teach us a true art of life.[9]

This indication finds echoes in and supports arguments made elsewhere that we must strengthen our ego in the right way, the healthy way. The imps, both Luciferic and Ahrimanic, on either shoulder that each one of us bears can cease to be a concern for us. For as a consequence of our knowledge of them we are able to harness their perfectly legitimate forces in ways that are altogether beneficial, and this not only for furtherance on our own path to perfection but also for that of our neighbours on theirs.

Our eyes, it is said, are the windows of our soul, and the abstract term 'eye contact' is employed in common speech nowadays. Rudolf Steiner extended this notion in typical fashion:

> Kind words spoken to us have a direct effect on us, just as colour affects our eyes directly. The love living in the other's soul is borne into your soul on the wings of the words. This is direct perception; there can be no question here of interpretation.[10]

'Christ knows us'[11]

Those who tread the path of personal development and take into account this statement will, without difficulty, arrive at the consideration that almost every person we meet can say it too. In other words, when we exercise our ego-sense whilst confronting another individual, we are, either consciously or unconsciously, seeking to espy—and acknowledge—the Christ in that person. At some time or other on our path of development it will be incumbent on us to strive to discern in each fellow human being a *representative of mankind* in the sense of the quotation at Note 7.

With enhanced sensitivity acquired as a consequence of gaining whatever knowledge of the temperaments we are able to accumulate, we shall be able to perceive how a particular individual is succeeding in maintaining a balance between the Luciferic and Ahrimanic attributes inbuilt into his or her whole being. We shall then be in a position to determine, in terms of sympathy and antipathy in the light of our understanding of human nature in all its rich variety, how best to approach and interact with that individual.

With this attitude permeating our behaviour, we soon come to a realistic notion of two representatives of humanity encountering what is Christlike in each other. This whole blend of feeling, thinking and willing should endure as a fundamental mood of the soul during any encounter with other human beings, whether meaningful and significant or fleeting and inconsequential. But at least the lowest rung in the ladder of social interaction, namely, common courtesy and consideration for others, will have been mounted.

We know very well that we should love our neighbour as ourselves—and even more than that. Such love is capable of sustaining us after death as well as during life, and this many people instinctively realize. Rudolf Steiner pointed out on many occasions that the sources of love are inexhaustible, and that love is perhaps the only 'commodity' that can be freely given without its reserves becoming depleted. Love figures large in scriptural and devotional works, and many of the meditational verses that he gave also concern this most basic of human needs and gifts. Its vital role in the whole of human existence does not need to be laboured, but the following quotation from one of his lectures deals not only with love but the entire human condition, as woeful now as it has ever been.

> All love, lower and higher, is the breath of the gods. Wisdom underlies the world, but love evolves. Wisdom is the guide of love. Just as all wisdom is born out of error, so does love struggle to the heights only out of conflict. Wisdom in animals is instinctive, but conscious in us — we have to strive for it. Self-love must become love of all, for only then will evil be overcome.[12]

Notes and References

Thematic quote: Steiner, R., *Verses and Meditations*, p. 141.

Chapter 1   The General and the Particular

1. Steiner, R., *The Four Temperaments*, Lecture, 9 January 1909.
2. Childs, G., *Understand Your Temperament!*, Appendix II and *passim*.
3. Of these researchers, only Eysenck took the notion of the four temperaments seriously. See Eysenck, H.J., *Fact and Fiction in Psychology*, Penguin Books, 1965.
4. See Childs, G., op cit., for further discussion.
5. Steiner, R., *The World as the Working of Balance*.
6. Steiner, R., *Occult Science, passim*.

Chapter 2   Physiognomy and Psychology

1. Shakespeare, W., *Julius Caesar*, Act 1, Scene 2.
2. Steiner, R., *The Effects of Spiritual Development*, p. 59.
3. Steiner, R., *Von Seelenrätseln*, Rudolf Steiner Verlag (GA 21).
4. Childs, G., *Understand Your Temperament!*, Appendix II.
5. Steiner, R., *The Effects of Spiritual Development*, p. 60.
6. Dickens, C., *A Christmas Carol*.
7. Steiner, R., *The Effects of Occult Development*, p. 46 and *passim*.
8. Steiner, R., 'The Nature of Egotism', in *Metamorphoses of the Soul*.
9. Steiner, R., *The Inner Realities of Evolution*, p. 58f.
10. Steiner, R., *The Effects of Spiritual Development*, p. 45.

Chapter 3 The World as a Work of Art

1. Steiner, R., *Man as Symphony of the Creative Word*, Lecture 1.
2. Steiner, R., *Goethe's Conception of the World*.
3. Eliot, R., & de Paoli, C., *Kitchen Pharmacy*, Chapmans, 1991, p. 92.
4. Luke, D., *Goethe*, Penguin Books, 1964, p. xxix.
5. Steiner, R., *Goethe's Conception of the World*, p. 37f.
6. Childs, G., *Understand Your Temperament!*
7. This sign is also associated with life. Scorpio, the Scorpion's sting is indicative of the sting of death (1 Corinthians 15:55), but death to the world of sense implies birth into the supersensible world of spirit. The symbol of this kind of resurrection or rebirth is the Eagle, with its ability to soar to great heights. Legend has it that it is the only creature that is able to look directly at the sun, but even the eagle must return to earth sooner or later.
8. Lehrs, E., *Man or Matter*, Chapter XIX; Steiner, R., *The World as the Working of Balance*.
9. Steiner, R., *Man as Symphony of the Creative Word*, Chapter IX.
10. Steiner, R., *Four Seasons and the Archangels; The Cycle of the Year*.
11. Steiner, R., *Truth-Wrought Words*, p. 61.

Chapter 4 A Meditative Approach to Self-knowledge

1. Steiner, R., *Verses and Meditations*, p. 49.
2. Steiner, R., *Man as Picture of the Living Spirit*.
3. For further discussion see Childs, G., *An Imp on Either Shoulder*.
4. Goethe, J. von, *Faust*, Part 1, Scene 3.
5. Steiner, R., *Initiation, Eternity and the Passing Moment*.
6. Steiner, R., *Verses and Meditations*, p. 59.
7. Childs, G., *An Imp on Either Shoulder*, passim.
8. Childs, G. & S., *The Journey Continues...*, passim.
9. Steiner, R., *The Four Seasons and the Archangels; Spiritual Hier-*

archies; *Calendar of the Soul;* and *The Cycle of the Year*—these are all rich sources of information and inspiration.
10. Steiner, R., *Theosophy,* Chapter 3.
11. Steiner, R., *The Spiritual Hierarchies,* Chapter 2 and *passim.*
12. Steiner, R., 'The Nature of Egotism', Lecture 5 in *Paths of Experience, Metamorphoses of the Soul,* Vol. 2.
13. Steiner, R., *Anthroposophical Ethics,* Lecture 3.
14. Lehrs, E., *Man or Matter.*
15. Lehrs, E., ibid., Chapter VII.

Chapter 5 Equalizing Positive and Negative

1. Steiner, R., 'Man: Positive and Negative', Lecture VIII in *Paths of Experience, Metamorphoses of the Soul,* Vol. 1.
2. Because of Rudolf Steiner's usage of the terms *positive* and *negative* within this particular context, it is absolutely imperative that there be no confusion in the reader's mind. For instance, these terms are employed in their usually understood sense in a sister publication, namely, Florin Lowndes's book *Enlivening the Chakra of the Heart,* Sophia Books, 1998 (see, for example, p. 90).
3. Steiner, R., ibid.
4. Childs, G., *Understand Your Temperament!*
5. Steiner, R., 'Man: Positive and Negative', Lecture VIII in *Paths of Exprience, Metamorphoses of the Soul,* Vol. 1, RSP.
6. Berger, P.L. & Luckmann, T., *The Social Construction of Reality,* Penguin 1971.
7. Steiner, R., *The Four Temperaments.*
8. Steiner, R., *Discussions with Teachers,* Lecture 1.
9. Steiner, R., 'Man: Positive and Negative', Lecture VIII in *Paths of Experience, Metamorphosis of the Soul,* Vol. 1.

Chapter 6 Smoothing the Mixture

1. Steiner, R., *Soul Economy and Waldorf Education,* Lecture XVI. This quote is from Albert Steffen's report on the Course

which was published as *Lectures to Teachers*, p. 104.
2. Steiner, R., *Man as a Picture of the Living Spirit*, Lecture, 2 September 1923.
3. Steiner, R., *Verses and Meditations*, p. 197.
4. Steiner, R., *Occult Science – An Outline*, chapter IV.
5. Steiner, R., *Life Beyond Death; Life Between Death and Rebirth*.
6. For further discussion at introductory level, see Childs, G., *From Birthlessness to Deathlessness*, Fire Tree Press.
7. Steiner, R., 'The Nature of Egotism', Lecture 5 in *Paths of Experience, Metamophoses of the Soul*, Vol. 2.
8. Steiner, R., *Truth-Wrought Words*, p. 17.
9. Steiner, R., *Study of Man*, Lecture V.
10. Steiner, R., *The World of the Senses and the World of the Spirit*.
11. Steiner, R., *Anthroposophical Ethics*, pp. 60–62.
12. Steiner, R., *The Effect of Occult Development*, Lecture 3.

Chapter 7 The Greeks Had a Word for It

1. Steiner, R., *The Four Temperaments*.
2. Steiner, R., *Verses and Meditations*, p. 49.
3. Steiner, R., ibid., p. 55.
4. Steiner, R., *How to Know Higher Worlds*, Chapter 4.
5. Steiner, R., *Christ in Relationship with Lucifer and Ahriman*, passim.
6. Steiner, R., 'The Nature of Egotism', Lecture 5 in *Paths of Experience, Metamorphoses of the Soul*, Vol. 2.
7. Steiner, R., *Verses and Meditations*, p. 191.
8. Steiner, R., *Preparing for the Sixth Epoch*, 1957.
9. Steiner, R., *The Four Temperaments*.
10. Steiner, R., *Towards Imagination*, p. 54.
11. Steiner, R., *Verses and Meditations*, p. 223.
12. Steiner, R., *The Origins of Suffering. The Origin of Evil, Illness and Death*.

Select Bibliography

Titles by Rudolf Steiner

Anthroposophical Ethics, Anthroposophical Publishing Co., 1928.
Calendar of the Soul, Rudolf Steiner Publishing Co., 1948.
Christ in Relationship to Lucifer and Ahriman, Anthroposophic Press, 1978.
Cycle of the Year, Anthroposophic Press, 1989.
Discussions with Teachers, Rudolf Steiner Press, 1967.
Effects of Spiritual Development, Rudolf Steiner Press, 1978.
Four Seasons and the Archangels, Rudolf Steiner Press, 1990.
Four Temperaments, Rudolf Steiner Publishing Co., 1944.
Goethe's Conception of the World, Anthroposophical Publishing Co., 1928.
Initiation, Eternity and the Passing Moment, Anthroposophic Press, 1985.
Inner Realities of Evolution, Rudolf Steiner Publishing Co., 1953.
Knowledge of the Higher Worlds and its Attainment, G.P. Putnam's Sons, 1923, now *How to Know Higher Worlds*, Rudolf Steiner Press, 1997.
Lectures to Teachers, Anthroposophic Press, 1931, now *Soul Economy and Waldorf Education*, Anthroposophic Press, 1986.
Life Beyond Death, Rudolf Steiner Press, 1995.
Life Between Death and Rebirth, Anthroposophic Press, 1968.
Man as Picture of the Living Spirit, Rudolf Steiner Press, 1972.
Man as Symphony of the Creative Word, Rudolf Steiner Publishing Co., 1945.
Paths of Experience, Metamorphoses of the Soul, Rudolf Steiner Press, 1992.
Metamorphoses of the Soul, Rudolf Steiner Publishing Co., n.d.
Occult Science – an Outline, Anthroposophic Press, 1939.

Origins of Suffering. The Origin of Evil, Illness and Death, Steiner Book Centre, 1980.
Preparing for the Sixth Epoch, Anthroposophic Press, 1957.
Spiritual Hierarchies and the Physical World, Anthroposophic Press, 1996.
Theosophy, Anthroposophic Press, 1947.
Towards Imagination, Anthroposophic Press, 1990.
Truth-Wrought Words, Anthroposopic Press, 1979.
Von Seelenrätseln, Rudolf Steiner Verlag, 1990 (GA 21).
World as the Working of Balance, Rudolf Steiner Press, 1948.
World of the Senses and the World of the Spirit, Anthroposophic Press, 1979.
Verses and Meditations, Rudolf Steiner Press, 1979.

Books by other authors

Berger, P.L. & Luckmann, T., *The Social Construction of Reality*, Penguin, 1971.
Childs, G., *An Imp on Either Shoulder*, Fire Tree Press, 1995.
Childs, G., *From Birthlessness to Deathlessness*, Fire Tree Press, 1996.
Childs, G., *Understand Your Temperament!*, Sophia Books, 1995.
Childs, G. & S., *The Journey Continues...*, Sophia Books, 1998.
Dickens, C., *A Christmas Carol*.
Eliot, R., & de Paoli, C., *Kitchen Pharmacy*, Chapmans, 1991.
Eysenck, H.J., *Fact and Fiction in Psychology*, Penguin Books, 1965.
Goethe, J. von, *Faust*, Part 1, Scene 3.
Lehrs, E., *Man or Matter*, Faber and Faber, 1951.
Lowndes, F., *Enlivening the Chakra of the Heart*, Sophia Books, 1998.
Luke, D., *Goethe*, Penguin Books, 1964.